후다닥 하룻밤에 끝내는

NEW SMART

영어회화 대표문장 2500

CHRIS SUH

MENTORS

후다닥 하룻밤에 끝내는
New SMART
영어회화 대표문장 2500

2024년 8월 7일 인쇄
2024년 8월 14일 발행

지 은 이 Chris Suh
발 행 인 Chris Suh
발 행 처 **MENTORS**
경기도 성남시 분당구 분당로 53번길 12 313-1
TEL 031-604-0025 FAX 031-696-5221
mentors.co.kr
blog.naver.com/mentorsbook
* Play 스토어 및 App 스토어에서 '멘토스북' 검색해 어플다운받기!
등록일자 2005년 7월 27일
등록번호 제 2022-000130호
I S B N 979-11-988743-0-6
가 격 15,600원(MP3 무료다운로드)

PREFACE

「패턴+숙어」의 조합

모국어가 아닌 제 2외국어로서 영어를 배우는 사람들이, 미국에 가서 직접 부딪히면서 영어를 배우지 않는 한, 가장 효율적인 학습방법은 영어회화의 패턴을 집중적으로 익히는 것이고 그런 다음 그 패턴에 넣을 흔히 말하는 숙어라는 표현들을 왕창 습득해야 된다. 이렇게 필자는 기존 책에서 누누히 강조하였다. 그래서 〈영어회화 공식 303〉이나 〈영어회화 공식패턴 3300: 기본-핵심-응용〉 등의 패턴 책을 발행하였으며 또한 이 패턴들에 넣어 문장을 만들 표현들을 〈네이티브가 쓰는 쉬운 영어 이젠 나도 써본다 1, 2권〉에 수록한 바 있다.

기초자는 처음부터 「패턴+숙어」의 조합에 낯설다

그렇다면 지금 이 책, 〈후다닥 하룻밤에 끝내는 영어회화 대표문장 2500〉은 어떤 성격, 어떤 부류에 속하는 교재일까··· 「패턴+숙어」의 조합은 무궁무진한 문장들을 만들어낼 수 있다. 하지만 영어회화 기초를 하는 사람들에게 처음부터 「패턴+숙어」의 조합으로 해서 영어문장들을 만들라고 하면 그 낯설음에, 자신없음에 금방 포기하기 쉽다. 이런 단점을 보완하기 위해서 바로 이 책은 나오게 된 것이다.

이책은 「패턴+숙어」의 조합에 익숙하도록 꾸며져

즉, 〈후다닥 하룻밤에 끝내는 영어회화 대표문장 2500〉은 「패턴+숙어」의 조합으로 만들 수 있는 문장 중에서 가장 대표적인 문장들을 알파벳 순으로 모아 놓았다. 이 문장들만 암기할 수 있다면 먼저 「패턴+숙어」의 방법을 이해하기 쉽고 그래서 「패턴+숙어」의 방법을 써서 더 많은 문장들을 새로 만들어낼 수 있는 노하우가 생기게 된다는 점이다. 예를 들어서 Do I have to~?(내가 ···을 해야 돼?)와 make a reservation(예약하다)을 조합해서 문장을 만들기보다 Do I have to make a reservation?를 기본적으로 익히고 들어가면 "아, 이렇게 조합하면 되는구나"를 느끼게 되고 이렇게 외워서 사용하다보면 다음 새로운 문장을 만드는데 도움이 된다는 말이다.

익숙해진 「패턴+숙어」의 조합으로 다양한 문장을 만들 수 있어

또한 이 책에는 「패턴+숙어」의 조합으로 해결되지 않은 Anything else?, No problem 등의 단문장, 그리고 I don't get it, I don't blame you와 같은 자주 쓰이는 빈출 표현들 또한 함께 수록하였다. 아무쪼록 이 책을 통해 영어회화의 최단 지름길인 「패턴+숙어」의 조합방법에 익숙해지고 어떤 상황 어떤 경우에서도 영어문장이 술술 입에서 나오게 될 것을 확신한다.

이 책의 특징

Common Sentences in English Conversation

1. 「패턴+숙어」의 조합에 익숙해지도록 영어회화의 기본표현들을 집중적으로 수록하였다.
2. 영어회화에서 많이 쓰이는 한 두단어로 된 문장들도 빠트리지 않고 싸그리 모았다.
3. 또한 좀 낯설지만 역시 많이 쓰이는 상당히 미국적인 영어 표현들 또한 함께 정리하였다.
4. 각 표현 아래에는 강의식으로 보충설명이나 추가 예문을 넣어서 초보자의 이해를 더욱 쉽게 도모하였다.
5. 모든 문장은 생동감 넘치는 원어민의 녹음이 되어 있어서 따라 읽으면서 실제 연습이 되도록 꾸며졌다.

이 책의 구성

Common Sentences in English Conversation

1. 총 2500 여개의 문장들이 알파벳 순서로 사전식으로 정리되어 있다.
2. 알파벳 구성은
   A–D,
   E–H,
   IJK,
   L–P,
   S–T,
   UW, 그리고
   Y으로 총 7파트로 대분되어 나뉘어져 있다.

3. 각 파트가 끝날 때는 Check It Out!이 있어 실제 영어회화에서 각 문장들이 어떻게 쓰이는지 보여주고 있다.

이책을 쉽게 보는 법

Common Sentences in English Conversation

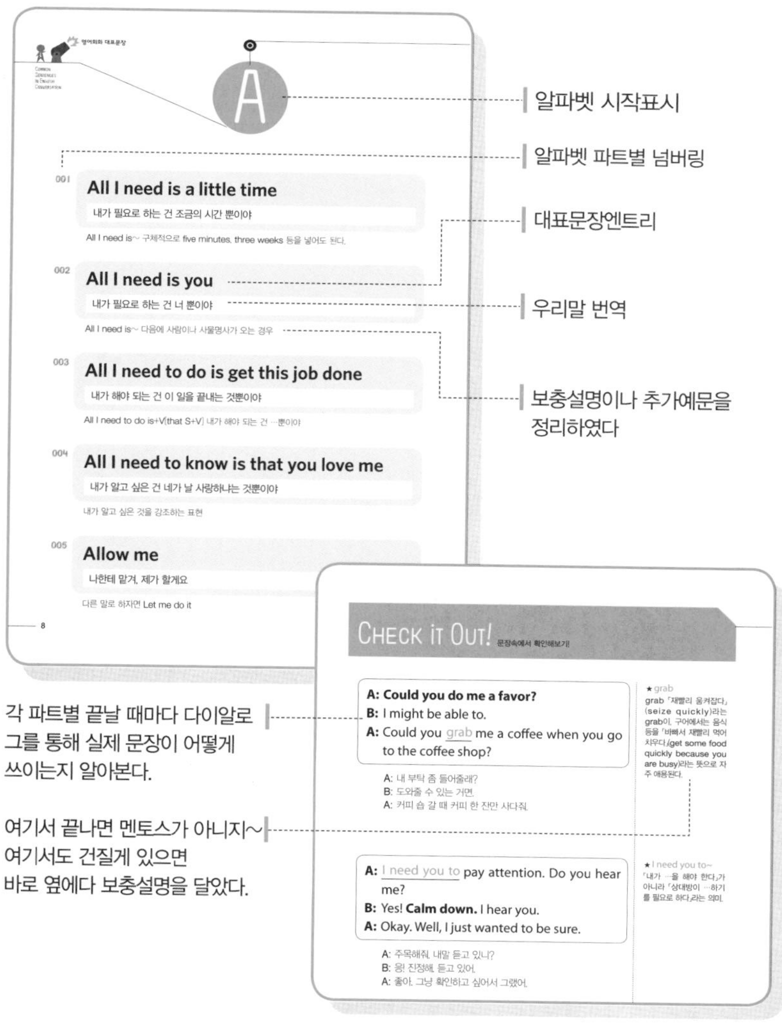

영어회화 대표문장
A
알파벳 시작표시
알파벳 파트별 넘버링
대표문장엔트리
우리말 번역
보충설명이나 추가예문을 정리하였다
001 All I need is a little time
내가 필요로 하는 건 조금의 시간 뿐이야
All I need is~ 구체적으로 five minutes, three weeks 등을 넣어도 된다.
002 All I need is you
내가 필요로 하는 건 너 뿐이야
All I need is~ 다음에 사람이나 사물명사가 오는 경우
003 All I need to do is get this job done
내가 해야 되는 건 이 일을 끝내는 것뿐이야
All I need to do is+V[that S+V] 내가 해야 되는 건 …뿐이야
004 All I need to know is that you love me
내가 알고 싶은 건 네가 날 사랑하냐는 것뿐이야
내가 알고 싶은 것을 강조하는 표현
005 Allow me
나한테 맡겨, 제가 할게요
다른 말로 하자면 Let me do it
8
CHECK IT OUT! 문장속에서 확인해보기!
A: Could you do me a favor?
B: I might be able to.
A: Could you grab me a coffee when you go to the coffee shop?
A: 내 부탁 좀 들어줄래?
B: 도와줄 수 있는 거면.
A: 커피 숍 갈 때 커피 한 잔만 사다줘.
★ grab
grab 「재빨리 움켜잡다」(seize quickly)라는 grab이, 구어에서는 음식 등을 「바빠서 재빨리 먹어치우다」(get some food quickly because you are busy)라는 뜻으로 자주 애용된다.
A: I need you to pay attention. Do you hear me?
B: Yes! Calm down. I hear you.
A: Okay. Well, I just wanted to be sure.
A: 주목해줘. 내말 듣고 있니?
B: 응! 진정해. 듣고 있어.
A: 좋아. 그냥 확인하고 싶어서 그랬어.
★ I need you to~
「내가 …을 해야 한다」가 아니라 「상대방이 …하기를 필요로 하다」라는 의미.
각 파트별 끝날 때마다 다이알로그를 통해 실제 문장이 어떻게 쓰이는지 알아본다.
여기서 끝나면 멘토스가 아니지~ 여기서도 건질게 있으면 바로 옆에다 보충설명을 달았다.

CONTENTS

Common Sentences in English Conversation

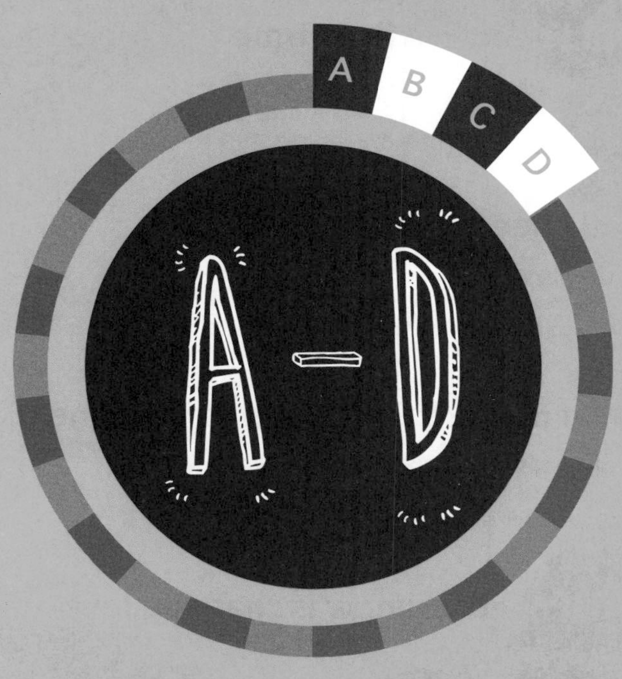
A
B
C
D
A-D

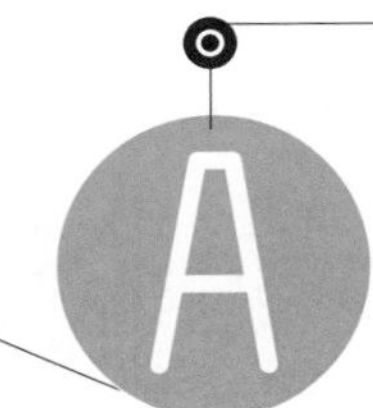

001 **All I need is a little time**

내가 필요로 하는 건 조금의 시간 뿐이야

All I need is~ 구체적으로 five minutes, three weeks 등을 넣어도 된다.

002 **All I need is you**

내가 필요로 하는 건 너 뿐이야

All I need is~ 다음에 사람이나 사물명사가 오는 경우

003 **All I need to do is get this job done**

내가 해야 되는 건 이 일을 끝내는 것뿐이야

All I need to do is+V[that S+V] 내가 해야 되는 건 …뿐이야

004 **All I need to know is that you love me**

내가 알고 싶은 건 네가 날 사랑하냐는 것뿐이야

내가 알고 싶은 것을 강조하는 표현

005 **Allow me**

나한테 맡겨, 제가 할게요

다른 말로 하자면 Let me do it

006 **Any messages for me?**

메시지 온 것 있어요?

앞에 Is there~이 생략된 것

007 **Any questions?**

뭐 질문 있어요?

뭐 다른 질문있냐고 할 때는 Any other questions?

008 **Anything else?**

뭐 다른 것 있어?

뭐 새로운 거 있어?는 Anything new?

009 **Anything to declare?**

(세관)신고할게 있습니까?

원래는 Do you have anything to declare?

010 **Anything wrong?**

뭐 잘못된거라도 있어?

011 **Anything you say**

뭐든지 말만해(다 들어주겠다)

I don't believe anything you say하면 상대방을 다 못믿겠다는 말

012

Are you all set to go to school?

학교갈 준비 다 됐어?

be (all) set to+V는 …할 준비가 되어 있다

013

Are you alright?

괜찮겠어?

alright은 all right의 구어체 표현

014

Are you available now?

지금 시간 돼?

오늘 저녁 시간 돼?는 Are you available tonight?

015

Are you aware of its history?

그것의 내력을 알고 있어?

be aware of~는 …을 알고 있다

016

Are you aware of what's going on with Jim?

짐이 어떻게 지내는지 알아?

be aware of~뒤에는 의문사절이 올 수도 있다

017

Are you coming with us?

우리랑 같이 갈래?

함께 가자고 권유할 때

018 **Are you finished[done]?**

다했어?

거의 다했냐고 물어볼 때는 Are you almost done?

019 **Are you free in the afternoon?**

오후에 시간 돼?

여기서 free는 available과 같은 의미

020 **Are you going my way?**

같은 방향으로 가니?

상대방에게 그쪽으로 가냐고 물어볼 때는 Are you going that way?

021 **Are you going to be here on the weekend?**

주말에 여기 있을 건가요?

on the weekend는 주말에, on the weekends는 주말마다

022 **Are you insane?**

너 미쳤니?

insane은 out of one's mind와 같은 의미

023 **Are you interested in soccer?**

축구에 관심있어?

be interested in = have interest in

024 **Are you leaving so soon?**

벌써 가는 거야?

모임 등에서 일어나 나가는 사람에게 던지는 인사말

025 **Are you looking for anything in particular?**

뭐 특별히 찾고 있는게 있나요?

in particular는 특별히라는 의미

026 **Are you married?**

결혼했어?

027 **Are you okay?**

괜찮아?

okay 대신에 all right을 써도 된다.

028 **Are you out of your mind?**

너 제 정신야?

앞서 나온 Are you insane?과 같은 말

029 **Are you ready for our meeting?**

회의 준비됐어?

be ready for+N는 …에 준비되다라는 말

030 **Are you ready for that?**

그거 준비됐어?

031 **Are you ready to go?**

갈 준비됐어?

be ready to+V는 …할 준비가 되어 있다라는 말

032 **Are you ready to order now?**

지금 주문하시겠어요?

식당에서 웨이터가 주문받을 때

033 **Are you ready to talk about this?**

이거 지금 얘기할래요?

상대방과 얘기 나누고 싶을 때

034 **Are you saying it was an accident?**

그게 사고였다는거야?

Are you saying S+V?는 …라는 말야?라고 상대방의 말을 확인하는 문장

035 **Are you saying that you didn't?**

네가 안 그랬다는거야?

상대방이 뭔가 부정할 때

036 **Are you saying that you're not happy?**

행복하지 않다는 말야?

상대방이 불행하냐고 확인할 때

037 **Are you saying there's a problem?**

문제가 있다는거야?

뭔가 문제가 있는지 확인할 때

038 **Are you saying this is my fault?**

이게 내 잘못이라고 말하는거야?

이게 내 잘못이냐고 따지고 들 때

039 **Are you saying you want to stay together?**

함께 남고 싶다는 거야?

stay together는 함께 남다

040 **Are you saying you won't do it?**

너 그렇게 하지 않을거라는 거야?

won't의 발음은 [wount]이다.

041 **Are you serious?**

정말야?

상대방 말의 진의를 묻거나 놀라서 하는 말

042 **Are you still playing computer games?**

아직도 컴퓨터 게임하니?

컴퓨터 게임을 하다는 항상 복수를 써서 play computer games라 한다

043 **Are you still there?**

듣고 있는 거니?

전화영어로 아직 상대방이 전화를 끊지 않았는지 확인할 때

044 **Are you sure it's okay if we stay another day?**

우리가 하루 더 머물러도 정말 괜찮아?

Are you sure~?는 …해도 되는지 상대방에게 확인하는 말

045 **Are you sure you did it?**

정말 네가 그렇게 한거야?

상대방에게 진짜 그랬냐고 확인하는 문장

046 **Are you sure you want this?**

이걸 원하는게 맞아?

047 **Are you sure you'll be able to do it?**

정말 너 그거 할 수 있어?

네가 마음을 바꾸지 않을게 확실해?는 Are you sure you're not going to change your mind?

048

Are you sure you're okay?

정말 괜찮아?

상대방이 괜찮은지 확인하고 싶을 때

049

Are you sure?

정말야?

그게 정말 맞아?는 Are you sure about that?

050

Aren't you going to miss it?

그게 그립지 않겠어?

부정의문문으로 먹지 않을거야?는 Aren't you going to eat?

051

Aren't you happy about this promotion?

이번 승진이 기쁘지 않아?

be happy about은 …에 기쁘다

052

Aren't you nervous about having to go there?

거기 가는데 떨리지 않아?

be nervous about~은 …에 초조하다

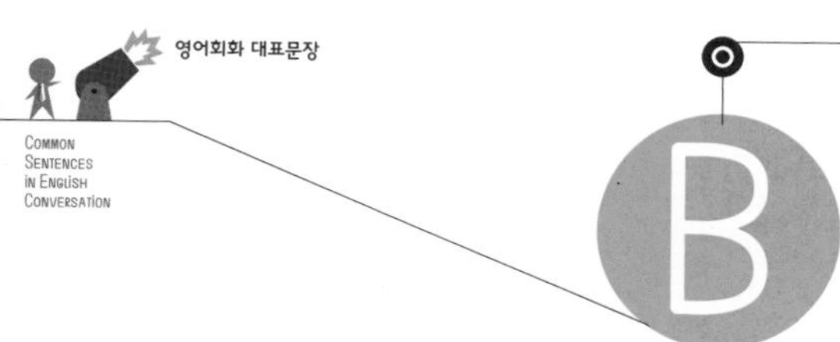

001

Be a good boy!

착하게 굴어!

나쁜 짓 하지 말라고 하는 말

002

Be careful

조심해

"그거 조심해"는 Be careful with it[that]

003

Be here at 7:40

7시 40분까지 여기에 와

be here는 come과 같은 말

004

Be honest

솔직해 봐

"솔직히 말해서"는 To be honest, "뒤통수 치지마"는 Don't go behind my back이라고 하면 된다.

005

Be my valentine

발렌타인 때 내 애인이 되어줘

발렌타인 데이에 나와 함께 있어달라고 할 때. "내 들러리가 되어줘"는 Be my best man

006
Be my guest

그럼, 그렇게 해

상대방의 요청을 허락할 때 쓰는 말로 Go ahead라고 해도 된다.

007
Be nice

점잖게 굴어

사람들을 잘 대해주라는 의미로 Be kinder라 해도 된다.

008
Be sure to check them all

반드시 그것들 다 확인해봐

Be sure to+V는 "반드시 …하라"고 말할 때

009
Be sure to come back by 7 o'clock

7시까지는 반드시 돌아와

뭘하든 7시까지는 돌아와 있으라는 말.

010
Be sure to do that

반드시 그렇게 해

"꼭 내게 이멜을 써라"고 할 때는 Be sure to email me

011
Beats me

내가 어떻게 알아

쉽게 말하면 I don't know, 어렵게 말하면 Search me

012 **Been there, done that**

(전에도 해본 것이어서) 뻔할 뻔자지

I have~가 각각 생략된 것으로 과거에 경험해본 것이라는 의미

013 **Behave yourself**

행동거지 조심해

행동거지 바르게 하라고 하는 말로 You need to beahve well

014 **Better late than never**

아예 안하는 거보단 늦는 게 나아

never보다는 later가 더 낫다는 말

015 **Better than nothing**

없는 것보다 낫네

앞에 It's가 생략되었으며 어떤 결과가 예상과 다르지만 그렇게 나쁘지 않다는 의미

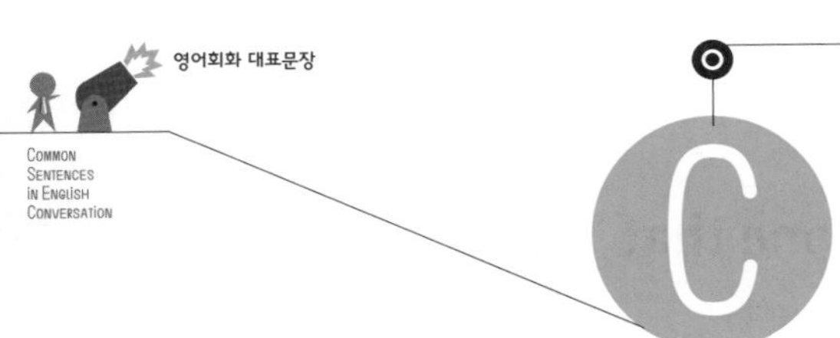

001

Calm down

진정해

Don't be upset, Take it easy, Settle down이라고 해도 된다

002

Can I ask you a favor?

부탁하나 해도 될까요?

Can you do something that will help me?라는 말로 Could you do me a favor?라고 해도 된다.

003

Can I ask you a question?

질문 하나 해도 돼?

I have a question for you라는 말로 Can I ask you a question about~?이라고 이어 말할 수 있다.

004

Can I ask you something?

뭐 좀 물어봐도 돼?

Let me ask you something이라고 해도 된다.

005

Can I bring this on the plane?

이거 비행기에 갖고 가도 돼나요?

bring sth on the plane은 비행기에 …을 갖고 타다

006 **Can I get you a cup of coffee?**

커피 한 잔 가져다 줄까?

Can I get you sth?은 상대방에게 …을 갖다줄까?라고 의사를 물어보는 문장.

007 **Can I get you a drink?**

뭔가 마실걸 줄까?

달리 I'll get you a drink라고 해도 된다.

008 **Can I get you something?**

뭐 좀 가져다 줄까?

가져다주거나 사다줄 때. "뭐 다른거 가져다줄까?"는 Can I get you something else?

009 **Can I hang around with you today?**

너랑 오늘 놀아도 돼?

hang around with sb는 …와 함께 놀다, 어울리다

010 **Can I help you with anything?**

뭐 좀 도와줄까?

그냥 Can I help you?라고도 많이 쓴다.

011 **Can I pay by credit card?**

신용카드로 결제할 수 있나요?

Let me pay for it with my credit card라고 해도 된다

012 **Can I talk to you for a second?**

잠깐 얘기 좀 할까?

I'd like to talk to you라는 말로 for a second는 줄여서 for a sec이라고 해도 된다.

013 **Can I try this on?**

이거 입어봐도 되나요?

try sth은 먹다, 시도하다, try sth on은 입어[신어]보다

014 **Can we keep this between us?**

이거 우리끼리 비밀로 할래?

keep sth between us는 …을 우리끼리 비밀로 하다

015 **Can you believe how much this is going to cost?**

아까 말한 게 얼마나 비싼 건지 아니?

Can you believe~?은 뭔가 놀라운 사실을 강조해서 전달하는 표현법

016 **Can you believe I finally did it?**

내가 마침내 그걸 했다는 게 믿겨져?

뭔가 대단한 일을 하고서 할 수 있는 말

017 **Can you believe she didn't know it?**

걔가 그걸 모르고 있었다는 게 믿겨져?

걔가 스트리퍼였다는 게 믿겨져?는 Can you believe she was a stripper?

018 **Can you believe this is already happening?**

벌써 이렇게 됐어?

달리 말하자면 I just can't believe this is happening, again(이런 일이 또 생기다니 믿을 수가 없어)

019 **Can you believe this[it]?**

믿겨져?

믿기지 않은 것을 간단히 this[it]으로 표현한 경우

020 **Can you come to the party this Friday?**

이번 금요일 파티에 올래?

Can you~?는 상대방의 의향이나 사정을 물어볼 때

021 **Can you do this for me?**

이것 좀 해줄래?

Could로 써서 Could you do it for me?라고 해도 된다.

022 **Can you give me a call tonight?**

오늘 밤에 전화해줄래?

give sb a call은 …에게 전화하다

023 **Can you give me a discount?**

깎아줄래요?

a 대신에 any를 써도 되며 현금으로 결제하면(for paying cash)이라는 어구를 붙여 써도 된다.

024 **Can you give me another chance?**

기회 한 번 더 줄래요?

give sb a chance는 …에게 기회를 주다

025 **Can you help me get dressed?**

옷 입는 거 좀 도와줄래?

help sb+V[help sb with sth]은 …가 …하는 것을 돕다

026 **Can you help me?**

도와줄래?

I don't know what I'm doing. Can you help me?는 어떻게 해야 할지 모르겠어. 도와줄테야?

027 **Can you meet me on Sunday?**

일요일날 만날래?

요일명 앞에는 전치사 on이 온다.

028 **Can you pay for dinner? I can't afford it**

저녁값 낼래? 내가 돈이 없어서

pay for sth은 …의 값을 치루다

029 **Can you please help me fix this problem?**

이 문제 푸는거 도와줄테야?

fix the problem은 문제를 풀다, 해결하다

030 **Can you tell me about it over the phone?**

그거 전화로 얘기해줄래?

전화 등의 통신망을 말할 때는 전치사 over를 쓴다.

031 **Can you tell me how to stop it?**

그걸 어떻게 멈추는 지 말해줄래?

tell sb how to+V는 …에게 …하는 법을 말하다

032 **Can you tell me how you feel?**

네 감정을 말해줄테야?

tell sb how S+V …가 어떠한지 …에게 말하다

033 **Can you tell me what happened?**

무슨 일인지 말해줄래?

"남편한테 무슨 일이 일어났는지 말해줄래?"는 Can you tell me what happened to your husband?

034 **Can you tell me what that is?**

저게 무언지 말해줄래?

035 **Can you tell me what's going on in there?**

거기에 무슨 일인지 말해줄래?

go on은 여기서 happen

036 **Can you tell me why not?**

왜 싫은지 말해줄래?

037 **Can you tell me why?**

이유를 말해줄래?

Can you tell me why S+V?의 형태를 쓸 수도 있다.

038 **Can you tell me your address?**

네 주소 좀 알려줘

tell me 다음에 사물명사가 바로 이어지는 경우

039 **Can't be beat**

최고다

defeat(…을 이기다), do better than(…보다 낫다)이라는 뜻을 지닌 동사 beat의 수동태를 이용한 구문

040 **Can't you wait just a little bit longer?**

좀 더 기다리면 안되겠어?

a little bit이나 a bit은 '조금'이라는 뜻으로 많이 쓰이는 표현이다.

041 **Catch you later**

나중에 보자

헤어질 때 하는 말로 I'll see you in the future라는 의미.

042 **Check it out!**

확인해봐!, 이것 좀 봐!

상대방의 주의를 끌 이것 좀 보라고 하거나 혹은 이거 확인해봐라는 의미

043 **Come again?**

뭐라구요?

잘 못들었을 때. I'm sorry? = Excuse me? = Pardon me? = Come again?

044 **Come on!**

서둘러!

어서 서둘러, 제발 그러지마, 자 덤벼 등의 다양한 의미로 쓰인다.

045 **Come over and see me sometime**

언제 와서 보자

come over는 come visit me라는 말로 "우리집에 들려"는 Come over to my place.

046 **Come to think of it**

생각해보니까 말야

뭔가 생각이 나서 말을 꺼낼 때로 Yes, now I remember라는 의미

047 **Coming through! Give me some room**

지나가게 좀 물러나줘

Excuse me. I need to get past you라고 해도 된다.

048

Could I be excused?

이만 일어나도 될까요?

답은 You're excused(그러세요. 그만 가봐)라 하면 된다.

049

Could you do me a favor?

제 부탁 좀 들어주시겠어요?

Could 대신 Would를 써도 된다.

050

Could you excuse me?

실례할게요

잠시 자리를 비울 때

051

Could you excuse us for a second?

자리 좀 비켜줄래요?

상대방에게 잠시 자리를 비켜달라고 할 때

052

Could you give me a hand?

나 좀 도와줄래?

give sb a hand는 도와주다라는 말

053

Could you please hurry?

좀 서둘러 줄래?

다음에 좀 급하다고 하면서 I'm in a bit of a rush라 말하면 된다.

054 **Could you repeat that?**

다시 말해줄래?

상대방이 한 말을 다시 한번 더 말해달라고 할 때

055 **Could you take a picture of us?**

우리 사진 좀 찍어줄래?

take a picture of sb는 …의 사진을 찍다

056 **Couldn't be better!**

아주 좋아!

부정어+비교어 = 최상급의 공식에 적용되는 표현

057 **Couldn't care less!**

알게 뭐람!

= I don't care = It means nothing to me

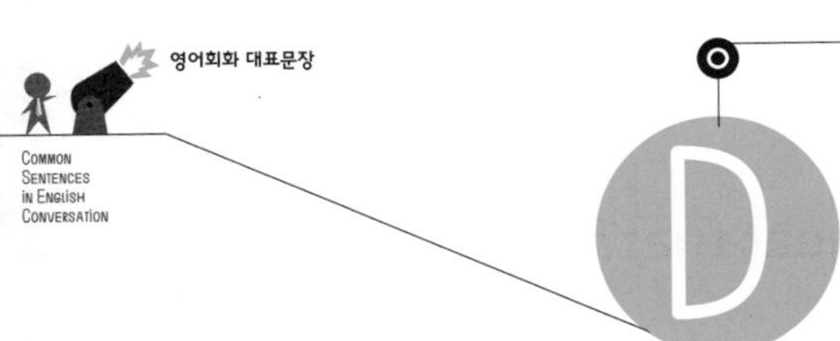

D

001 **Did you check with security?**

경비에게 확인했어?

여기서 security는 보안이 아니라 경비원을 말한다.

002 **Did you enjoy your trip?**

여행 즐거웠어?

enjoy one's trip은 여행을 즐겁게 하다

003 **Did you have a chance to check it?**

확인할 기회가 있었어?

have a chance to+V는 …할 기회가 있다

004 **Did you have a nice weekend?**

멋진 주말 보냈어?

월요일에 쓸 수 있는 인사말

005 **Did you hear that?**

너 그 얘기 들었니?

뭔가 새로운 소식을 전할 때 쓰는 표현으로 Did you hear that S+V?의 형태로 써도 된다.

006 **Did you know that?**

그거 알고 있었어?

know와 that 사이에 about을 넣어 Did you know about that?(그거에 대해 알고 있었어?)라고 해도 된다.

007 **Did you see any movies recently?**

최근에 뭐 영화본거 있어?

"액션 영화를 보다"는 see action movies

008 **Did you see that?**

봤지?, 내 말이 맞지?

단순히 Look at what just happened라고 쓰이기도 하지만 내 말이 맞았다(Look, I knew that would happen)라고 할 때도 쓰인다.

009 **Did you sleep well last night?**

간밤에 잘 잤어?

"수면장애가 있어"는 I haven't been able to sleep well

010 **Do I have to choose?**

내가 선택해야 돼?

Do I have to+V?는 내가 …해야 돼?냐고 묻는 문장

011 **Do I have to decide right now?**

지금 결정해야 돼?

012 **Do I have to make a reservation?**

예약을 해야 하나요?

make a reservation = reserve

013 **Do I have to remind you how serious this situation is?**

이 상황이 얼마나 심각한지 상기시켜줘야 돼?

Do I have to remind you how+형용사 S+V?는 "얼마나 …한지 내가 상기시켜줘야겠어?"

014 **Do I have to wait here until he drops by?**

걔가 들를 때까지 기다려야 돼?

drop by = drop in = stop by는 예고 없이 잠시 들르다

015 **Do I know you?**

저 아세요?, 누구시죠?

전에 (어디서) 만난적 있나요?(Have we met (somewhere) before?)와 같은 말

016 **Do I make myself clear?**

내 말 알아들었지?

앞서 말한 내용을 잘 이해했는지 물어보는 것으로 Have you understood?라는 말.

017 **Do we have to do this now?**

우리가 지금 이거 해야 돼?

뒤에 I haven't had my coffee yet(난 아직 커피도 못마셨는데) 등의 표현을 이어 쓰면 된다.

018 **Do we have to talk about this right now?**

지금 이 얘기를 해야 돼?

talk about sth은 …에 관해 이야기하다

019 **Do you accept credit card?**

신용카드 받아요?

"수표를 받다"는 accept[take] checks

020 **Do you believe in ghosts?**

유령이 있다고 생각해?

believe in~는 …가 있다고 믿다라는 말

021 **Do you feel like getting a drink?**

술 한잔 하고 싶어?

feel like ~ing는 …하고 싶다

022 **Do you get along well with your roommate?**

룸메이트랑 잘 지내니?

get along (with sb)는 (…와) 사이좋게 지내다

023 **Do you have a minute?**

시간 좀 있어?

시간이 있으면 Well yeah, sure, what's up?이라고 한다.

024 **Do you have a problem (with that)?**

(그게) 뭐 문제라도 있어?

"내게 뭐 불만이라도 있어?"는 Do you have a problem with me?

025 **Do you have another idea?**

그럼 좋은 방법이 있어?

다른 좋은 생각이 있는지 여부를 물어볼 때

026 **Do you have any hobbies?**

뭐 취미라도 있어?

Do you have any+N?는 혹시 …가 있어?라고 묻는 말

027 **Do you have any idea how dangerous those are?**

저것들이 얼마나 위험한 줄 알기나 해?!

"내가 얼마나 놀랐는지 알아?"는 Do you have any idea how scared I was?

028 **Do you have any idea how much that hurts?**

그게 얼마나 아픈지 알기나 해?

여기서 hurt는 자동사로 아프다

029 **Do you have any idea what happened to David last night?**

어젯밤에 데이빗에게 무슨 일이 있었는지 알아?

단순히 특정 정보를 물어볼 수도 있지만 문맥에 따라서는 상대방을 꾸짖을 때 사용되기도 한다.

030 **Do you have any idea what this means?**

이게 무슨 의미인지 알아?

"이게 나한테 무슨 의미인지나 알아?"는 Do you have any idea what this means to me?

031 **Do you have any idea what you just said?**

네가 방금 뭐라고 했는지나 알어?

"걔가 뭐라고 했는지 알아?"는 Do you have any idea what she said?

032 **Do you have any idea where she is?**

걔가 어디 있는지 알아?

Do you have any idea~ ? = Do you know~ ?

033 **Do you have any idea who did this?**

누가 이렇게 했는지 알아?

여기서 who는 주격

034 **Do you have any idea?**

뭐 좀 아는 게 있어?, 뭐 좋은 생각있어?

035 **Do you have any plans for tonight?**

오늘 밤 뭐 계획있어?

"저녁 식사 계획 뭐 있어?"는 Do you have any plans for dinner?

036 **Do you have any problem?**

뭐 문제라도 있어?

불확실하지만 상대방에게 뭔가 문제가 있어 보일때

037 **Do you have any questions for us?**

우리에게 무슨 질문이라도 있어?

038 **Do you have anything in mind?**

뭐 생각해둔 거라도 있어?

have sth in mind는 마음에 두다, 생각하다

039 **Do you have kids?**

애들은 있어?

호구조사용 표현

040 **Do you have the time?**

시간 좀 알려주시겠어요?

달리 말하면 What time do you have?, 참고로 Do you have time?은 시간있냐고 묻는 문장.

041 **Do you have time?**

시간 있어?

"커피 마실 시간 있어?"는 Do you have time for a coffee?

042 **Do you have to be here?**

여기 있어야 돼?

043 **Do you have to do that?**

그렇게 해야 돼?

044 **Do you have to go back to work?**

일하러 돌아가야 돼?

go back to work는 일하러 돌아가다, get back to work는 다시 일하다

045 **Do you have to stay?**

남아 있어야 돼?

046 **Do you have to work tonight?**

오늘밤 일해야 돼?

"오늘 밤 퇴근 후에는 뭐 할거야?"는 What are you doing after work tonight?

047 **Do you hear me?**

알았지?, 내말 듣고 있니?

자신이 한 말을 들었는지 듣고 있는지 확인하는 문장

048 **Do you know any good restaurants?**

좋은 식당 아는데 있어?

"이 근처에 좋은 식당 뭐 알아?"는 Do you know any good restaurants around here?

049 **Do you know anything about that?**

그거에 대해 아는 거 있어?

"차 수리하는거 아는 거 있어?"는 Do you know anything about repairing the car?

050 **Do you know each other?**

둘이 아는 사이니?

"걔 알아?"는 Do you know her?

051 **Do you know how long I've wanted this?**

내가 이걸 얼마나 오랫동안 원했는지 알아?

how long과 과거부터 현재까지의 기간을 나타내는 현재완료는 잘 어울린다.

052 **Do you know how old she is?**

걔가 몇 살인지 알아?

053 **Do you know how to fix it?**

그거 어떻게 고치[사용하]는지 알아?

know how to+V는 …하는 법을 알다

054 **Do you know how to use it?**

그걸 어떻게 사용하는지 알아?

055 **Do you know that?**

그거 알고 있어?

"어떻게 그걸 안거야?"는 How do you know that?

056 **Do you know the shortest way to the mall?**

쇼핑몰로 가는 지름길 알아?

the shortest way to~는 …로 가는 지름길

057 **Do you know what I mean?**

내 말 알아 들었어?

058 **Do you know what I'm saying?**

내가 하는 말 알겠어?, 무슨 소리인지 알겠어?

앞서 나온 Do I make myself clear?와 같은 맥락

059 **Do you know what just happened?**

방금 무슨 일이 일어났는지 알아?

뭔가 새롭고 놀라운 소식을 전할 때

060 **Do you know what you're doing?**

네가 뭘 하고 있는지 알아?

상대방에게 충고할 때

061 **Do you know where the subway station is?**

전철역이 어디에 있는 지 알아?

길을 물을 때 자주 사용하는 표현

062 **Do you know who did that?**

누가 그랬는지 알아?

063 **Do you know why I'm laughing?**

내가 왜 웃고 있는지 알아?

064 **Do you like it?**

좋아?, 맘에 들어?

it 대신에 that을 써도 좋다.

065 **Do you like Korean food?**

한국 음식 좋아해?

외국인에게 써볼 수 있는 문장

066 **Do you like playing computer games?**

컴퓨터 게임 하는 거 좋아해?

like 다음에는 명사 혹은 ~ing 혹은 to+V가 온다.

067 **Do you like singing?**

노래부르는 거 좋아해?

"저런 음악 좋아해?"는 Do you like that kind of music?

068 **Do you like to play golf?**

골프치는 거 좋아해?

play 다음에는 관사없이 운동명을 쓴다.

069 **Do you like working there?**

거기서 일하는 거 좋아해?

070 **Do you mean he might like me?**

걔가 날 좋아할 지도 모른단 말야?

상대방 얘기를 다시 확인할 때는 Do you mean S+V?

071 **Do you mean that?**

정말야?

상대방의 말이 진심인지 여부를 물어볼 때

072

Do you mean you won't be coming over for dinner?

저녁먹으러 오지 않을거란 말야?

come over for dinner는 저녁먹으러 오다[들르다]

073

Do you mind closing the door behind you?

나갈 때 문 좀 닫을래?

"내일 나 좀 태워줄 수 있어?"는 Do you mind picking me up tomorrow?

074

Do you mind if I sit here for a sec?

여기 잠시 앉아도 돼?

"여기서 담배 펴도 돼?"는 Do you mind if I smoke in here?

075

Do you mind turning the TV off?

텔레비전 좀 끌래?

Do you mind~ 다음에는 ~ing 혹은 if S+V가 이어진다.

076

Do you mind?

그만해줄래?, 괜찮겠니?

상대의 언행에 화가 나서 그만해줄래(Please stop that), 혹은 뭔가 허락을 구할 때(Is it OK if this is done) 괜찮겠니?라는 의미로 쓰인다.

077

Do you need a day off?

하루 쉬어야 돼?

a day off는 하루 휴가

078 **Do you need a ride?**

태워다 줄까?

상대방에게 차로 태워주겠다고 할 때

079 **Do you need an answer right now?**

지금 당장 답변이 필요해?

080 **Do you need anything else?**

뭐 다른 거 필요해?

더 필요한게 없으면 No. That's all I need라고 하면 된다.

081 **Do you need me to go with you?**

함께 가줄까?

need sb to+V는 …가 …하는게 필요하다

082 **Do you need more time?**

시간 더 필요해?

083 **Do you need my help?**

내가 도와줄까?

my 대신 some을 써도 된다.

084 **Do you need to go now?**

지금 가야 돼?

Do you need~ 다음에는 명사나 to+V가 온다.

085 **Do you need to take a rest?**

쉬어야 돼?

take a rest = get some rest 좀 쉬다

086 **Do you really like Chris?**

크리스를 정말 좋아해?

087 **Do you take checks?**

수표를 받나요?

take checks = accept a check 수표를 받다

088 **Do you think I should call?**

내가 전화해야 될 것 같아?

should는 반드시 …해야 한다라기 보다는 …하는게 나을거야에 해당

089 **Do you think it's too expensive?**

너무 비싸다고 생각해?

090 **Do you think she likes me?**

걔가 날 좋아하는 것 같아?

091 **Do you think there's a chance to do it?**

그걸 할 기회가 있을 것 같아?

there's chance to+V는 …할 기회가 있다

092 **Do you think this color suits me?**

이 색깔이 내게 맞는 것 같아?

suit는 정장, …에게 맞다, suite는 호텔의 스위트룸

093 **Do you think this will do any good?**

이게 도움이 될 것 같아?

"아무 도움이 안될거야"는 It won't do any good

094 **Do you think we should go there?**

우리가 거기 가야 된다고 생각해?

should = ought to, have to = must

095 **Do you think you can do that for me?**

네가 날 위해 그걸 할 수 있을 것 같아?

do sth for sb는 …을 위해 …을 하다

A-D | E-H | I-K | L-P | S-T | U-W | Y

096 **Do you understand, Mike?**

이해하겠어, 마이크?

097 **Do you want a date Saturday?**

토요일날 데이트할래?

date는 데이트 혹은 데이트하는 상대

098 **Do you want a refund?**

환불원해요?

"환불해주세요"는 I'd like to get a refund, please

099 **Do you want me to check again?**

확인 더 해볼까요?

check again = double check

100 **Do you want me to give you a ride to the office?**

사무실까지 태워다줄까?

give sb a ride to+장소는 …을 …에 차로 태워다주다

101 **Do you want me to go get them for you?**

내가 가서 그것들 가져올까요?

go get은 go to get에서 to가 생략된 경우

102 **Do you want me to quit?**

그만 두라고요?

담배를 끊다는 quit cigarettes, 이 일을 그만둘거야는 I'm going to quit this job

103 **Do you want me to teach you?**

내가 가르쳐줄까?

want sb to+V는 …가 …하기를 원하다

104 **Do you want some?**

좀 먹을래?

"더 들래"는 Do you want some more?, "좀 더 들어"는 Have some more

105 **Do you want to buy me a drink?**

술한잔 사줄래?

buy sb a drink는 술한잔 사주다

106 **Do you want to come along?**

같이 갈래?

get along은 사이좋게 잘 지내다, come along (with sb)은 같이 가다

107 **Do you want to come see a movie with us?**

와서 우리랑 같이 영화볼래?

역시 come see는 come to see에서 to가 생략된 것

108
Do you want to go get a drink?

가서 한 잔할래?

get a drink는 한잔 하다

109
Do you want to go out with me?

나랑 데이트하고 싶어?

go out with sb는 단순히 함께 외출하다 혹은 데이트하다

110
Do you want to hold?

기다리시겠어요?

전화온 사람에게 잠깐 기다리겠냐고 의사를 물어볼 때

111
Do you want to meet me there?

거기서 날 만날래?

112
Do you want to talk about it?

그거에 대해 얘기하고 싶어?

talk about sth with sb는 …와 …대해서 얘기하다

113
Do you want us to come back later?

우리가 나중에 다시 올까?

come back later는 나중에 다시오다

114 **Do you want us to leave the room?**

우리가 나갈까?

leave for+장소는 …을 향해 출발하다, leave+장소는 …을 떠나다, 나가다

115 **Do you want us to take you home?**

제시카, 우리가 집에 데려다 줄까?

take sb to+장소 혹은 take sb+부사의 패턴

116 **Does it make any sense?**

그게 말이나 돼?

말이 될 때는 It makes sense to me, 말이 안될 때는 It doesn't make any sense

117 **Does it matter?**

그게 문제가 돼?, 그게 무슨 상관이야?

= Is it important?, …가 중요해는 Does it matter that S+V?

118 **Does she still feel bad?**

걘 아직도 기분이 그래?

feel bad는 기분이 안좋다, feel good은 기분이 좋다, feel better는 기분이 나아지다

119 **Does size matter?**

크기가 문제돼?

여기서 matter는 자동사로 중요하다, 문제되다

120 **Does that work for you?**

괜찮겠어?

sth works for sb는 …가 …에게 괜찮은지를 묻는말로, "난 괜찮아"는 It works for me

121 **Doesn't matter. I can decide later**

상관없어. 나중에 결정하면 돼

맨 앞에 주어 'I'가 생략된 경우

122 **Don't sweat it**

걱정마

너무 걱정을 하고 있는 사람에게. = Don't be stressed

123 **Don't be mad at me**

내게 화내지마

be mad at sb …에게 화를 내다

124 **Don't be nervous**

초조해하지마

125 **Don't be scared**

겁먹지마

scare는 타동사로 겁주다. 따라서 겁먹다는 be scared

126

Don't be so hard on yourself

너무 자책하지마

= Don't give yourself too hard a time

127

Don't be sorry

미안해하지마

상대방에게 미안해하지 말라고 위로 할 때

128

Don't be too hard on me

나 좀 못살게 굴지마

= Stop being so unkind to me

129

Don't disappoint me

날 실망시키지마

= Don't let me down

130

Don't do that!

그러지마!

"내게 다신 이러지마"는 Don't do this to me, again

131

Don't even think about it

절대 안돼

경고로 Don't do it이라는 의미. …할 생각은 꿈도 꾸지마는 Don't even think about ~ing

132

Don't ever try to do it

절대로 그러지마

ever는 부정문에서 at any time이라는 의미

133

Don't feel so bad about it

너무 속상해하지마

feel so bad about~는 …에게 무척 속상해하다

134

Don't forget to bring your girlfriend for the party

파티에 여자친구 데려오는거 잊지마

Don't forget to+V는 잊지 말고 …해라

135

Don't forget to buy milk at the store

가게에서 우유사오는거 잊지마

136

Don't forget to clean your room

방청소하는거 잊지마

clean one's room은 방을 청소하다

137

Don't forget to get me a present

내게 선물 사주는거 잊지마

get sb sth은 …에게 …을 사주다, 갖다주다

138 **Don't forget to invite us to the wedding**

우리 결혼식에 초대하는거 잊지마

invite sb to+이벤트는 …을 …에 초대하다

139 **Don't get angry with me!**

내게 화내지마!

get angry with sb는 …에게 화를 내다

140 **Don't get me wrong**

오해하지마

Don't take this wrong, but~는 오해하지마, 하지만…

141 **Don't get upset!**

화내지마!

upset은 화내다도 되지만 걱정한다는 의미도 된다.

142 **Don't give it a second thought**

걱정하지마

second 대신에 another를 써서 Don't give it another thought라고 해도 된다.

143 **Don't give me a hard time**

날 괴롭히지 마

give sb a hard time은 …을 괴롭히다, 힘들게하다

144

Don't give me that!

그런 소리마, 그따위 소리하지마

좀 적나나하게 말하자면 Don't give me that shit!

145

Don't give up

포기하지마

"너무 쉽게 포기하지마"는 Don't give up too easily, "당장 때려쳐"는 Give it up

146

Don't let her drink anymore!

걔 술 더 못 마시게 해!

let sb+V는 …가 …하도록 하다로 걔 운전시키지마는 Don't let her drive

147

Don't let her go

걔 못가게 해

148

Don't let him fool you

걔한테 속지마

fool은 동사로 놀리다, 속이다

149

Don't let it bother you

그딴 일로 신경쓸 필요없어

쉽게 말하면 Don't think about it

150 **Don't let it happen again**

다신 그러지마

대답은 I won't let it happen again

151 **Don't say a word**

한마디도 하지마

알았다면 비밀을 꼭 지킬게라고 하려면 I won't say a word

152 **Don't take it personally**

기분 나쁘게 받아들이지마

Don't get angry about this와 같은 말

153 **Don't tell me it doesn't matter**

상관없다고 말하지마

Don't tell me S+V는 "설마 …는 아니겠지"

154 **Don't tell me what to do**

나한테 이래라 저래라 하지마

= You can't control me

155 **Don't waste your time**

시간 낭비하지마

= It's worthless. "남의 시간 축내지마"는 Don't waste my time

156 **Don't worry about it**

그거 걱정마

"걱정마, 그럴 수도 있어"라고 위로하려면 Don't worry about that. That happens

157 **Don't you know he's a heartbreaker?**

걔가 바람둥이인지 몰랐어?

Don't you know S+V?는 놀람의 문장으로 =I can't believe that you didn't get that information

158 **Don't you know?**

몰랐어?

Don't you see?는 "모르겠어?"라는 말로 This won't help, don't you see?

159 **Don't you remember?**

기억안나?

"성탄절에 내게 준거야. 기억안나?"는 You got me this for Christmas. Don't you remember?

160 **Don't you see?**

모르겠어?, 그거 몰라?

Don't you know?와 차이점을 기억해둔다.

161 **Don't you think it's a little too early?**

좀 이르다고 생각되지 않냐?

Don't you think S+V? …인 것 같지 않아? 강조하거나 혹은 질책할 때

162 **Don't you think it's kind of selfish?**

좀 이기적인 것 같지 않니?

kind o f = sort of = 약간, 좀

163 **Don't you think it's time you went home?**

벌써 집에 늦은 것 같지 않아?

it's time S+V는 이미 …했어야 했는데 하지 못하고 있다는 뉘앙스

164 **Don't you think so?**

그렇게 생각되지 않아?

"왜 그렇게 생각해?"는 What makes you think so?

165 **Don't you think this is a little extreme?**

이거 좀 너무 지나치다고 생각하지 않아?

166 **Don't stay away so long**

자주 좀 와

= Let's meet again very soon

167 **Don't work too hard**

너무 무리하지마

글자 그대로 무리하지마 혹은 헤어지면서 하는 인사말

CHECK IT OUT! 문장속에서 확인해보기!

A: Could you do me a favor?
B: I might be able to.
A: Could you grab me a coffee when you go to the coffee shop?

A: 내 부탁 좀 들어줄래?
B: 도와줄 수 있는 거면.
A: 커피 숍 갈 때 커피 한 잔만 사다줘.

★ grab
grab 「재빨리 움켜잡다」(seize quickly)라는 grab이, 구어에서는 음식 등을 「바빠서 재빨리 먹어 치우다」(get some food quickly because you are busy)라는 뜻으로 자주 애용된다.

A: I need you to pay attention. Do you hear me?
B: Yes! **Calm down.** I hear you.
A: Okay. Well, I just wanted to be sure.

A: 주목해줘. 내말 듣고 있니?
B: 응! 진정해. 듣고 있어.
A: 좋아. 그냥 확인하고 싶어서 그랬어.

★ I need you to~
「내가 …을 해야 한다」가 아니라 「상대방이 …하기를 필요로 하다」라는 의미.

A: Do you have time for a coffee?
B: Sure.
A: Let's go to the coffee shop across the street.

A: 커피 한잔 할 시간 있어요?
B: 물론이죠.
A: 길 건너 커피 숍에 갑시다.

★ Sure
단독으로 쓰이는 것으로 「가벼운 Yes나 Of course」라고 생각하면 된다.

A: You should work things out with her.
B: Why does everyone think she is not to blame?
A: **Don't get me wrong.** I know she made a mistake.

A: 그 여자와의 문제를 해결하는 게 좋아.
B: 왜 모두들 그 여자한테는 잘못이 없다고 생각하는거지?
A: 오해하지 마. 나도 그 여자가 실수했다는거 알아.

★ work things out
여기서 work~out은 solve로 생각하면 된다.

A: Will I see you at the party tonight?
B: Absolutely! I wouldn't miss it for anything.
A: Okay, **catch you later.** Bye!

A: 오늘 밤 파티에 올거야?
B: 당연하지! 무슨 일이 있더라도 가야지.
A: 좋아. 그때 보자. 안녕!

★ I wouldn't miss it for anything
miss는 「놓치다」라는 뜻의 동사로, 「무슨 일이 있어도」(for anything) 그 파티(it)를 놓치지 않겠다, 즉 「피티에 꼭 가겠다」는 말

A: Could you give me a hand?
B: What do you need?
A: I need help setting up the computer.

A: 절 좀 도와줄래요?
B: 뭐가 필요한데요?
A: 컴퓨터를 설치하는데 도움이 필요해서요.

★ I need help~ing
「…하는데 도움이 필요하다」는 말로 help 다음에 ~ing 형태를 이어 쓰면 된다.

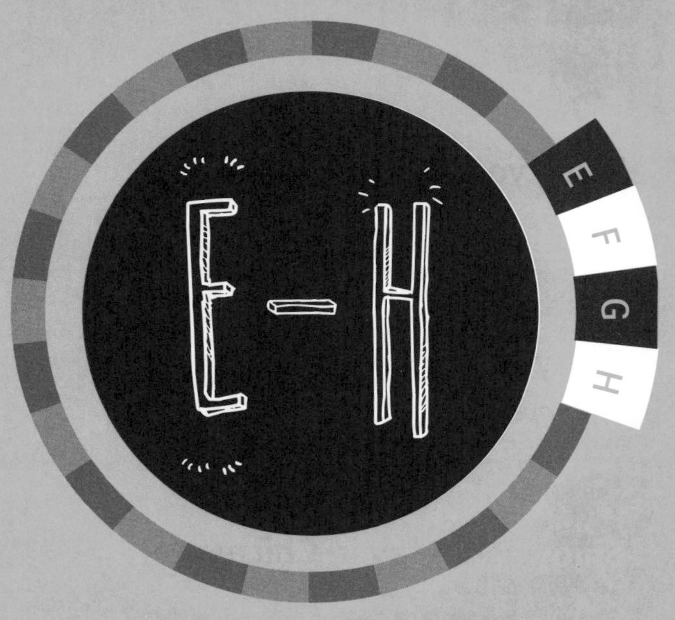
E-H
E
F
G
H

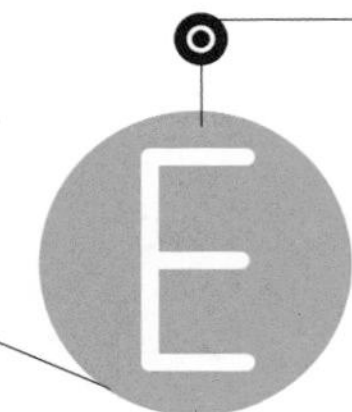

001

Easy does it

천천히 해, 진정해

Easy는 천천히, 조심조심(이사할 때), Ease up은 진정해, 그리고 easygoing person은 성격이 느긋한 사람

002

Enjoy your day off

잘 쉬어

쉬는 날인줄 알았던 동료가 출근했을 때는 Isn't this your day off?

003

Enjoy your meal!

식사 맛있게 해!

"배고파 뭐든지 먹겠어"는 I could eat a horse, 상대방이 적게 먹을 때는 You eat like a bird

004

Enjoy your stay in Chicago

시카고에서 즐겁게 보내세요

여행객이나 관광객에게 할 수 있는 문장

005

Enjoy yourself

재미있게 보내

= Have a good time

006 **Excuse me for being late**

늦어서 미안해

excuse sb for ~ing …가 …한거를 용서하다

007 **Excuse me, I didn't hear you well**

미안하지만 잘 못들었어요.

Excuse me는 여기서 "미안"이라는 말

008 **Excuse me, I seem to have lost my way**

실례합니다, 제가 길을 잃은 것 같아요

말을 걸 때의 Excuse me, lose one's way는 길을 잃다 = get lost

009 **Excuse me, there's a call on another line**

실례지만 다른 전화 와 있어요

a call on another line은 다른 전화가 걸려온 것을 의미

010 **Excuse me, what did you say?**

미안하지만 뭐라고 말했어?

What did you say? = Say what? = Say it again?

001 **Feel free to ask anything you want**

뭐든지 원하는거 물어봐

feel free to+V는 언제든 …해 = Go ahead and V~

002 **Feel free to come over to my place**

어려워 말고 집에 들러

소유격+place = house

003 **Feel free to drop by anytime**

언제든 편하게 들러

drop by = drop in = stop by 예고없이 잠깐 들르다

004 **Feel free to take a look around**

어려워말고 둘러봐요

둘러봐도 되냐고 물어보려면 Would you mind if I took a look around?

005 **Feel free to pick out whatever you need**

원하는 거 아무거나 골라

pick out = choose

006

Feel free to stay here as long as you like

계시고 싶을 때까지 마음놓고 머무르세요

as long as S+V …하는 한(기간의 의미는 없고 조건의 의미)

007

Fill it up, please

가득 채워주세요

주유소 용어. "고급유로 가득채워주세요"는 Fill it up with permium

008

For what?

뭐 때문에?

For what? = Tell me the reason. What for?는 왜?

009

Forget (about) it

됐어, 괜찮아

= Don't think about that anymore

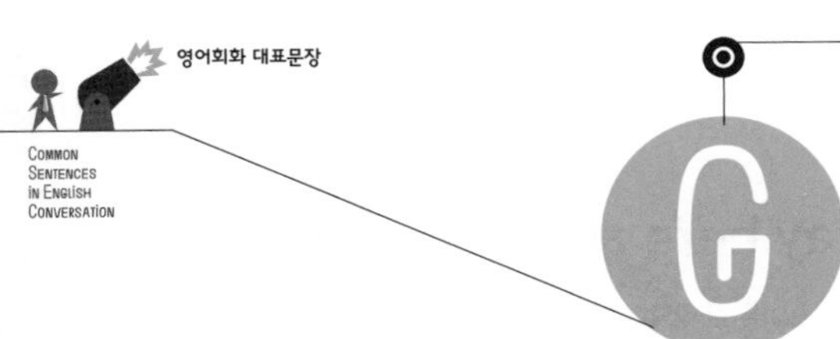

001 **Get back to me**

나중에 연락해

get back to sb 정보나 어떤 답을 주기 위해 나중에 얘기[전화]하다. "그건 나중에 얘기하자"는 Get back to me on that, "나중에 연락할게"는 Let me get back to you

002 **Get dressed**

옷 입어

"옷을 벗다"는 get undressed

003 **Get in there**

거기로 들어가

"비켜!, 나 들어가야 돼!"는 Get out of my way! I've got to get in there!

004 **Get me something to write on**

메모할 것 좀 줘

something 위에다 쓰기 때문에 전치사 on이 온다.

005 **Get off at the third stop**

3번째 정거장에서 내려

버스나 기차처럼 승차좌석이 높은 경우에는 off나 on을 쓴다. 승용차의 경우는 get out[in]

006 **Get off my back**

나 좀 내버려둬

= Stop bothering me about something = Get your hands off me

007 **Get on the next bus**

다음 버스를 타세요

버스에 타다는 get on

008 **Get out of here!**

꺼져, 웃기지마!

말 그대로 여기서 없어져라 뜻 외에 상대방이 말도 안되는 말을 할 때

009 **Get out of my face**

(내 앞에서) 꺼져

= Get out of my way = Get away from me

010 **Get real!**

정신 좀 차리라구!

Get a life! 역시 정신차리고 제대로 살라고 할 때

011 **Get your act together**

기운내

흩어진 자신을 모으라는 말로 Pull yourself together이라고 해도 된다.

012

Give me a break

좀 봐줘, 그만 좀 해라

기회를 달라고 할 때 혹은 말도 안되는 말을 하는 상대방에게 귀찮게 좀 굴지마라는 의미.

013

Give me a call anytime

언제든(언제 한번) 전화해

"언제 한번 전화해"는 Give me a call sometime

014

Give me a minute. I'll go change my clothes

잠깐만. 가서 옷 좀 갈아입을게

change one's clothes는 옷을 갈아입다

015

Give my best to him

걔에게 내 안부 전해줘

네 가족들에게 내 안부 전해줘는 Give my best to your folks

016

Go ahead, help yourself. Take whatever you want

어서 편히 들어. 뭐든 다 갖다 먹어

Go ahead는 권유나 동의시 하는 말로 Go ahead and +V의 형태로도 쓰인다.

017

Go down the escalator and you're there

에스컬레이터를 타고 내려가면 바로예요

엘리베이터에서 Going up?하면 "올라가세요?," This is my floor는 "저 내려요"

018 **Go down the street and take your first left**

이 길을 가다 첫사거리에서 왼쪽으로 도세요

019 **Go for it**

한번 해봐

한번 해보라고 권유하는 것으로 Try it and you may succeed

020 **Go straight along the street**

길따라 쭉 가세요

"두 블럭 직진하세요"는 Go straight 2 blocks

021 **Good for you!**

잘됐네!

= It was great that it happened to you. "내게 잘된 일이지"는 Good for me

022 **Good job**

잘했어

You did a good job의 줄인 문장으로 = Well done. Super job

023 **Good luck finding a girlfriend!**

여자 친구찾는데 행운이 있기를!

Good luck ~ing하면 …하는 행운이 있기를 바래

024 **Good luck on the project**

그 프로젝트 잘되기를 바래

Good luck on[with] sth~ …가 잘되기를 바래

025 **Good luck with that!**

그거 잘 되기를!

026 **Good to see you!**

만나서 반가워!

"야, 안녕, 반가워"는 Hey, how are you? It's good to see you.

027 **Guess what?**

그거 알아, 저기 말야

You know what?과 같은 표현으로 = I heard some interesting things

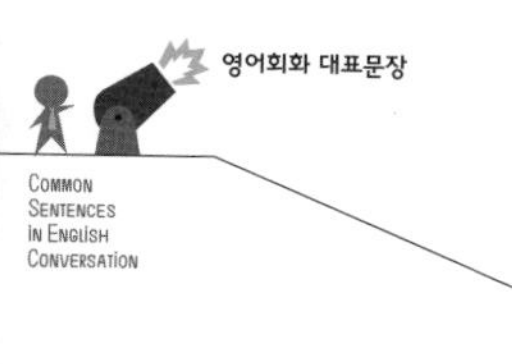

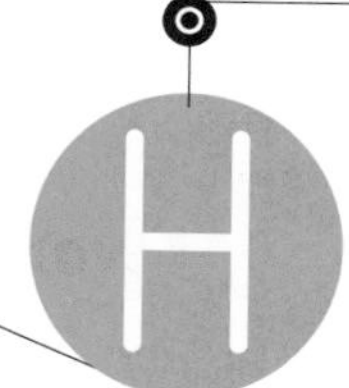

001
Hang in there
끝까지 버텨!

어려움에 처한 사람을 격려할 때 = Be strong and don't give up

002
Happy anniversary!
기념일 축하해!

기념일 인사는 Happy+기념일!

003
Happy Chusok!
추석 즐겁게 보내!

004
Hard to believe, isn't it?
믿기 어렵지, 그렇지?

앞에 It is~가 생략된 경우

005
Have a great honeymoon
멋진 신혼여행보내

Have a nice[good]+(시간, 기간관련) 명사!는 멋진 …을 보내!

006 **Have a nice day at work**

직장에서 즐거운 하루 보내요

at work는 근무중, 퇴근후는 after work

007 **Have a nice stay in New York**

뉴욕에 계시는 동안 즐거운 시간 되세요

008 **Have a nice trip!**

즐거운 여행 되세요!

"비행기 여행이 즐거우시길!"이라고 할 때는 Have a nice[good] flight!

009 **Have a nice weekend!**

주말 잘 보내!

금요일 오후에 꼭 하게 되는 인사말

010 **Have fun!**

재미있게 보내!

"재미있었어?"는 Did you have fun?

011 **Have you been thinking about my proposal?**

내 제안 생각해봤어?

과거부터 지금까지 생각한 것으로 현재완료 진행형을 쓴 경우

012 **Have you ever been to Disneyland?**

디즈니랜드에 가본 적 있어?

Have you (ever) been to+장소명사?는 …에 가본 적이 있어?

013 **Have you ever heard of that?**

그 얘기 들어본 적 있어?

014 **Have you ever thought about being there for her?**

걔를 위해 거기 갈 생각해본 적 있어?

Have you been thinking about~이 현재완료 진행형인 반면 이 문장은 그것의 현재완료형을 쓴 경우

015 **Have you ever thought of that?**

그거 생각해본 적이 있어?

of 대신 about을 써도 된다.

016 **Have you ever tried sushi?**

스시를 먹어본 적 있어?

try+음식명사는 …을 먹어보다

017 **Have you finished the project you started?**

시작한 프로젝트 끝냈어?

finish+N[~ing]는 …을 끝내다. "걔가 일을 끝냈는지 알아볼게"는 I'll check if he's finished working.

018 **Have you had your wisdom teeth pulled out?**

사랑니 뽑았어?

have sth+pp의 형태로 다른 사람이 sth을 pp했다는 말

019 **Have you made a hotel reservation?**

호텔 예약을 해본 적 있어?

make a reservation은 reserve

020 **Have you run the marathon before?**

전에 마라톤 뛰어본 적 있어?

과거의 경험을 물어보는 현재완료

021 **Have you seen my camera?**

내 카메라 봤어?

뭔가 물건을 찾으면서 물어볼 때 긴요한 문장

022 **Have you thought about counseling?**

카운셀링 생각해본 적 있어?

think about[of]+N[~ing]는 …을 생각하다

023 **He didn't show up**

걘 오지 않았어

약속한 장소에 나타나는 것은 show up

024 **He is looking at a site on the internet**

인터넷 사이트를 보고 있어

025 **He is not in at the moment**

지금 안계시는데요

be not in at the moment 지금 자리에 없다

026 **He makes me happy**

걔 때문에 내가 행복해

make[get]+목적어+형용사[pp]하게 되면 목적어를 "…하게 만들다"라는 의미로 특히 기쁘게 하다, 화나게 하다처럼 감정적인 표현을 할 때 사용된다.

027 **He may come here first**

걔가 제일 먼저 여기 올지 몰라

아직 잘 모르는 이야기를 할 때는 may[might]+V

028 **He must be with a client**

그는 고객과 함께 있어요

must be~는 …임에 틀림없다고 자신있게 추측할 때

029 **He said hello to you**

걔가 네게 안부 전해달래

say hello[hi] to sb는 …에게 안부인사를 하다

030

He told me to save my money

걔는 나보고 돈을 절약하라고 했어

tell sb to+V는 …에게 …하라고 말하다

031

He took a day off

갠 하루 쉬어

take[get] a day off는 하루 쉬다

032

He won't be able to meet you here today

갠 오늘 여기서 널 만날 수 없을거야

can의 미래형은 will be able to+V

033

He won't let me in

갠 날 들여보내주지 않을거야

let sb in은 …을 안에 들어오게 하다

034

He's already made up his mind

갠 이미 마음을 결정했어

make up one's mind는 decide. 또한 여기서 He's~는 He has~

035

He's away on vacation

갠 휴가중이야

be on leave라 해도 된다.

036

He's better than you think

걔는 네가 생각하는 거 이상야

037

He's gone for the day

그분은 퇴근하셨어요

Let's call it a day[night] = We're done for the day

038

He's got a big mouth

걘 입이 가벼워

has가 …을 갖고 있다라는 의미일 때에 한해서 has = has got

039

He's so eager to learn English

걔는 영어를 배우려고 열 올리고 있어

be eager to+V = be dying to+V = can't wait to+V = 몹시 …하고 싶다

040

He's upset about me

걘 내게 화났어

be upset about~ 다음에는 사물도 온다.

041

He's waiting for me at a restaurant

걘 식당에서 나를 기다리고 있어

wait for sb는 …을 기다리다

042

He's working now

걘 지금 일하고 있어

043

Help yourself to the buffet

찬장에 있는거 마음껏 들어

Help yourself는 마음껏 들라는 말로 먹는 대상을 적으려면 Help yourself to the cake, Help yourself to whatever's in the fridge라고 하면 된다.

044

Help yourself

갖다 드세요

= Take as much food as you want

045

Here are the papers you asked for

네가 부탁했던 서류 여기 있어

"내가 약속한 콘서트 티겟야"는 Here are the tickets to the concert that I promised.

046

Here you go

여기 있어

047

Here's good news for you

네게 좋은 소식있어

Here's sth for sb의 형태

048

Here's my business card

여기 내 명함요

business card는 명함

049

Here's something for you

여기 네게 줄거야

"이건 널 위한 조그만 것이야"는 Here's a little thing for you.

050

Here's something I got to tell you

네게 할 말이 있어.

Here's something~다음에 S+V가 나오는 패턴

051

Here's the deal

이렇게 하자, 이런 거야

= I'm going to tell you everything. "이렇게 되는거야. 열심히 일하면 성공할거야"는 Here's the deal. If you work hard, you are going to be successful.

052

Here's to you!

당신을 위해 건배!

"당신의 건강을 위하여"는 Here's to your health!

053

Here's your bill

여기 계산서입니다

식당영어.

054

Here's your passport

여기 여권있습니다

공항영어

055

He's always saying nice things about you

갠 항상 너에 대해 좋게 말해

say nice things about sb는 …에 대해 좋게 말하다

056

Hit the road!

출발하라고!

슬랭으로 hit the road는 뭔가 출발하다, 시작하다

057

Hold the line

(끊지말고) 기다리세요

전화영어

058

Hold your horses

서두르지 말고 기다려봐

서부시대 마차를 세울 때 어떻게 하는지 생각해보면 된다.

059

Hope you can make it

네가 올 수 있기를 바래

주어 'I'가 생략된 문장이고, make it은 (어떤 모임이나 목적지에) 도착하다

060 **How about another cup of coffee?**

커피 한 잔 더 들래?

How about sth?은 상대방에게 sth를 권유할 때

061 **How about going out for dinner?**

저녁 먹으러 나갈까?

How about ~ing?는 상대방에게 …하자고 권유할 때

062 **How about I give you a ride home?**

집에 태워다 줄까?

How about S+V는 상대방에게 …하면 어떻겠냐고 권유할 때

063 **How about now?**

지금은 어때?

"내일 저녁은 어때?"는 How about tomorrow evening?

064 **How about some dessert?**

디저트 좀 들래요?

디저트를 권할 때

065 **How about that?**

그건 어때?

How about that!(느낌표에 주목)하게 되면 "거 근사한데!," "그거 좋은데!," "잘됐군!"

066 How about we go to the movies tonight?

오늘 저녁 영화가는거 어때?

"네 아파트에서 만날까?"는 How about we meet at your apartment?

067 How about we talk about this over dinner?

저녁하면서 이 문제 얘기해보면 어때?

talk about sth over dinner[lunch] 저녁[점심]하면서 …을 얘기하다

068 How about you?

네 생각은 어때?

상대방의 의견을 물을 때

069 How're you doing?

안녕?, 잘지내?

What are you doing?은 너 뭐하는거야?라는 질책

070 How can I be sure?

내가 어떻게 확신할 수 있겠어?

be sure= be certain

071 How can I ever repay you?

어떻게 다 보답을 해야할지?

repay는 되갚다, 보답하다

072
How can I help you?

뭘 도와드릴까요?

서비스 정신이 돋보이는 문장

073
How can I tell?

내가 어찌 알아?

내가 알 수 없다는 말로 = What way could I be sure?

074
How can you be so confident?

어떻게 그렇게 자신있는거야?

How can you be so+형용사?의 패턴

075
How can you be so sure?

어떻게 그렇게 확실할 수 있어?

How can you be so sure S+V?의 형태도 쓰인다

076
How can you believe that?

어떻게 그걸 믿을 수 있어?

077
How can you do this to me?

어떻게 나한테 그럴 수 있어?

do this to sb는 …에게 그렇게 하다

078

How can you not trust me?

어떻게 나를 안 믿을 수가 있어?

How can you not+V?는 어떻게 …하지 않을 수 있어?

079

How can you say it is meaningless?

어떻게 그게 의미없다고 말할 수 있어?

상대방의 말에 발끈하면서 던질 수 있는 문장

080

How can you say that it doesn't matter?

어떻게 그게 상관없다고 말할 수 있어?

matter는 중요하다, 상관있다라는 동사

081

How can you say that?

어떻게 그렇게 말할 수 있어?

= I don't agree with what you said

082

How come we never talked like this before?

어떻게 우리가 전에 이 얘기를 안한거야?

How come S+V?는 한마디로 Why~의문문과 같다

083

How come you didn't tell me?

어째서 내게 말하지 않았어?

084 **How come you never said anything to me?**

왜 내게 한마디도 안 했던거야?

"어떻게 내게 얘기를 안한거야?"는 How come you never told me that?

085 **How come you're late?**

왜 이렇게 늦은거야?

How about~과 달리 How come~다음에는 무조건 S+V의 형태를 붙이면 된다.

086 **How come you're so weird?**

어째서 넌 그렇게 이상하냐?

weird는 이상한, 이상한 사람은 weirdo

087 **How come you're still at a job that you hate?**

왜 네가 싫어하는 직장에 아직도 다녀?

088 **How come?**

왜?, 어째서?

How come?은 단독으로 쓰일 수도 있으며 Why?, Why is that?과 같은 의미

089 **How could I have done that?**

내가 왜 그랬을까?

자신의 과거행동을 후회하면서 하는 말

090

How could this happen?

어떻게 이런 일이?

"어떻게 이런 일이? 너무 불공평하다는 말야"는 How could this happen? I mean, this is so unfair!

091

How could you do something like that?

넌 어떻게 그와 같은 짓을 할 수 있는거야?

do something like that 그와 같은 짓을 하다

092

How could you do that?

어떻게 그럴 수 있어?

= Why did you do that? 그리고 어떻게 내게 그럴 수 있어?는 How could you do this to me[us]?

093

How could you let this happen?

어떻게 이런 일이 일어나도록 놔뒀어?

let this happen은 이런 일이 일어나도록 놔두다

094

How could you treat him like that?

어떻게 걜 그렇게 대할 수 있어?

treat sb like that은 …을 그런 식으로 대하다

095

How dare you insult me!

감히 나를 모욕하다니!

How dare you+V~!는 어떻게 네가 …을 할 수가 있냐라는 뜻 = I'm very angry because of your actions. 참고로 How dare you!는 네가 뭔데!, 네가 감히!라는 의미

096 **How did it go?**

어떻게 됐어?, 어땠어?

= Did you have a good time?, How did it go with+N? …는 어떻게 됐어?

097 **How did it happen?**

이게 어떻게 된 거야?

= What was the cause of this thing?

098 **How did you do that?**

그걸 어떻게 한거야?

099 **How did you get a girl like that?**

어떻게 저런 여자를 만난거야?

100 **How did you get here so fast?**

여길 어떻게 그렇게 빨리 왔어?

get here = come

101 **How did you know we were here?**

우리 여기 있다는 걸 어떻게 알았어?

How did you know S+V?는 넌 …을 어떻게 알았어?

102

How do I get there from here?

여기서 거기에 어떻게 가?

get there = go

103

How do you do that?

어쩜 그렇게 잘하니?, 어떻게 해낸거야?

= Can you show me?

104

How do you feel?

기분이 어때?

How do you feel about~?는 …하는거 어때?

105

How do you know that?

어떻게 알았어?

106

How do you like my new suit?

내 새 옷은 어때?

How do you like+N?는 …가 어때?라며 상대방의 의견을 구하는 문장

107

How do you like that?

저것 좀 봐, 황당하지 않냐?, 어때?

= I'm really surprised it happened. = What is your opinion of that?

108 **How do you like the steak?**

스테이크 맛이 어때?

"이렇게 맛있는 스테이크는 처음이야"는 It's the juiciest steak I have ever eaten.

109 **How do you like your new computer?**

새로 산 컴퓨터 어때?

110 **How is that possible?**

어떻게 그럴 수가 있지?

= What make that happen?

111 **How long are you planning to stay in the US?**

미국엔 얼마나 머물 계획이세요?

be planning to+V는 …할 계획이다

112 **How long before you have to leave?**

네가 가기 전에 얼마동안이냐?

113 **How long does it take to finish it?**

이거를 마치는데 얼마나 걸려?

"그 일을 끝마치는데 얼마나 걸려?"는 How long does it take to finish the job?

114
How long does it take to get there?

거기 가는데 시간이 얼마나 걸려?

How long does it take to+V?는 …하는데 시간이 얼마나 걸려?

115
How long does it take to get to work from the station?

역에서 회사까지 얼마걸려요?

"출근하는데 얼마나 걸려?"는 How long does it take for you to get to work?

116
How long has he been here?

걔는 여기 얼마나 오래 있었는데?

기간을 말하는 How long~은 현재완료와 잘 어울린다.

117
How long has he been married?

결혼한 지 얼마나 됐어?

"우리가 결혼한지 몇 년 됐지?"는 How many years have we been married?

118
How long have you been dating him?

걔하고 데이트 얼마나 했어?

강조하기 위해 현재완료 진행형이 쓰인 경우

119
How long have you lived here?

여기 얼마나 오래 살았어?

120

How long is this going to take?

이게 얼마나 걸릴까?

121

How long?

얼마나 오래?

"얼마나 오래 전에?"는 How long ago?

122

How many calories have you had today?

오늘 칼로리를 얼마나 섭취했어?

How many/much+명사로 시작되는 문장. 수나 양이 얼마나 되는지 물어볼 때 쓰는 표현이다.

123

How many do you want?

몇 개를 원해?

124

How many drinks did you have last night?

지난 밤에 술을 몇 잔이나 마셨어?

125

How many kids are you going to have?

애를 몇이나 가질거야?

126

How many of you watched *Game of Thrones*?

너희들 중 몇이나 〈왕좌의 게임〉을 봤어?

How many of you+V? 너희들 중 몇이나 …을 했어?

127

How many people came to see you off?

널 배웅하러 몇 사람이 나온거야?

위의 경우처럼 How many+N가 주어로 쓰인 경우

128

How many stops are there to Gangnam Station?

강남역까지 몇 정거장입니까?

129

How many times did it happen?

몇 번이나 그랬는데?

How many times do[did] S+V?는 몇 번이나 …하니(했니)?라는 표현.

130

How many times do I have to say I'm sorry?

내가 몇 번이나 미안하다고 해야 돼?

How many times do I have to+V?는 몇번이나 내가 …라고 해야 되냐고 짜증내는 패턴.

131

How many times do I have to tell you!

내가 몇 번이나 네게 말해야 하니!

132 **How much can you afford to spend?**

예산은 얼마쯤 잡고 계시는데요?

How much는 셀 수 없는 양을 말하는 것으로 How much 다음에 오는 명사는 주로 How much time, How much money 정도이다.

133 **How much did it cost you?**

얼마 주고 샀어?

sth cost sb~는 …가 …를 주고 …을 사다

134 **How much do I owe you?**

(식당이나 가게) 이거 얼마죠?

= What is the amount of money I should pay you?

135 **How much do you love your wife?**

네 아내를 얼마나 사랑해?

136 **How much do you need?**

얼마나 많이 필요해?

137 **How much does it cost?**

이거 가격이 얼마예요?

"너 그거 얼마주고 샀어?"는 How much did it cost you?

138 **How much further?**

얼마나 더 멀어?

How much+형용사비교급?

139 **How much is this dress?**

이 옷이 얼마예요?

140 **How much longer?**

얼마나 길게?

141 **How much more?**

얼마나 더?

142 **How much time do you need?**

얼마나 많은 시간이 필요해?

143 **How much time?**

얼마나 많은 시간을?

144 **How much?**

얼마예요?

= How much is it?

145 **How nice!**

와 좋아라!

"정말 무례하네!"는 How rude!

146 **How often did he do this?**

걔가 얼마나 자주 이걸 했어?

How often~의 경우는 빈도수를 묻는 구문

147 **How often did you see her?**

얼마나 자주 걔를 봤어?

148 **How often do you talk about her?**

얼마나 자주 걔 이야기를 해?

149 **How often does that happen?**

이런 일이 얼마나 자주 일어나?

150

How should I forget?

어떻게 잊겠어?

못잊겠다는 말

151

How should I get to Chicago?

시카고에 뭘 타고 가야 되지?

How should I get to+지명?은 어떻게, 즉 무슨 교통수단으로 …까지 가는지 물어볼 때

152

How should I put it?

뭐랄까?

put it = express, To put it simply[shortly/briefly]는 간단히 말하자면, Let's put it this way는 이렇게 표현해보자고

153

How soon can it be delivered?

그게 얼마나 빨리 배달되나요?

How soon~은 언제쯤 …할 수 있을까요?라는 의미로 앞으로 기다릴 시간이 얼마나 되는지 묻는 것으로 조동사 can과 자주 어울린다.

154

How soon do you expect him back?

걔 언제쯤 돌아올까요?

= What time do you expect him back?

155

How soon do you need it?

얼마나 빨리 필요해요?

156 **How soon will you be able to get here?**

언제쯤 여기에 도착할 수 있죠?

157 **How soon?**

얼마나 빨리?

How often?은 얼마나 자주?, How long?은 얼마나 오래?

158 **How was that?**

그거 어땠어?

How was+N?는 …가 어땠어?

159 **How was your date last night?**

지난 밤 데이트 어땠어?

160 **How was your day?**

오늘 어땠어?

늦은 오후나 저녁에 쓰는 표현으로 반드시 과거동사 was를 써야 한다.

161 **How was your trip?**

여행 어땠어?

"비행여행은 어땠어?"는 How was your flight?

162 **How would you like it if I told everyone that you were a gay?**

네가 게이라고 모두에게 말한다면 어떻겠어?

How would you like it if S+V?는 …한다면 어떻겠어?

163 **How would you like some ice cream?**

아이스크림 좀 먹을테야?

How would you like+N?는 …를 어떻게 해줄까?, …을 할래[먹을래]?

164 **How would you like to come by for a drink?**

술 한잔 하러 잠시 들를래?

How would you like to do~?는 어떻게 …할 거야?, …을 하자는 제안표현

165 **How would you like to get together?**

만나는 게 어때?

"한번 만나자. 다음주 금요일로 할까?"는 How would you like to get together? Say next Saturday?

166 **How would you like to go out on a date with me?**

나랑 데이트 할래?

go out on a date (with) = go out (with)는 …와 데이트하다

167 **How would you like to join me?**

나랑 같이 할래?

168 **How would you like to pay for that?**

그거 어떻게 계산하시겠습니까?

"괜찮으면 신용카드로 할게요"는 With my credit card, if it's all right.

169 **How would you like your steak?**

스테이크를 어떻게 해드릴까요?

170 **How's everything with you these days?**

넌 요즘 어때?

171 **How's it going?**

어때?

"새로운 일은 어떠니?"는 How's it going with your new job?

172 **How's that?**

그거 어때?, 어째서 그래?

"그거 어때? 나아졌어?"는 How's that? Is that better?

173 **How's the family?**

가족들은 다 잘 지내죠?

the 대신에 your를 써도 된다. 또한 "여름방학 어때?"는 How's your summer vacation?

CHECK IT OUT! 문장속에서 확인해보기!

A: How could you do something like that?
B: I promise I won't let it happen again.
A: How can I be sure?

A: 어떻게 그럴 수가 있죠?
B: 다신 그런 일 없을 거예요. 약속해요.
A: 그걸 어떻게 믿죠?

★I promise
I promise S+V는 「…을 약속하다」라는 의미

A: Hello. What would you like?
B: Regular unleaded. **Please fill it up.**
A: No problem. Do you want the car wash with that?

A: 안녕하세요. 어떻게 드릴까요?
B: 보통 무연휘발유로 가득 채워주세요.
A: 알겠습니다. 세차도 해드릴까요?

★No problem
감사에 대한 인사 외에도 상대방이 부탁하거나 사과할 때도 쓰인다.

A: Hi, folks. Here are your dinners. Who ordered the steak?
B: I did. Thank you very much. It looks delicious!
A: You're very welcome. **Enjoy your meal!**

A: 자, 여러분. 음식이 나왔습니다. 스테이크 시키신 분 누구죠?
B: 저요. 고마워요. 맛있겠는 걸요!
A: 별말씀을. 맛있게 드세요!

★I did
I ordered란 말씀

A: How long does it take to finish it?
B: Unfortunately, I think that it's going to be another ten minutes or so.
A: I hope it won't be much longer than that.

A: 그거 끝내는 데 시간이 얼마나 걸리니?
B: 안됐지만 10분쯤 더 걸릴 것 같은데.
A: 그 이상 걸리지 않았으면 좋겠다.

★or so
or so 시간이나 거리 등 수량 뒤에 와서 「…쯤」, 「…가량」이란 의미. 단수명사 뒤에는 or two를 쓰기도 한다.

A: Get out of here!
B: I'm sorry, but let me explain why I did it.
A: I really don't have time to listen to you now.

A: 그만 나가봐!
B: 미안해, 하지만 내가 왜 그랬는지 설명할게.
A: 지금은 네 얘기를 들을 시간이 정말 없다니까.

★have time to~
「…할 시간이 있다」라는 뜻의 표현으로, have the time하게 되면 시간이 몇 시인지를 물어보는 어구가 된다.

A: Feel free to give me a call if you have any questions.
B: Thanks, I probably will. This software manual is very confusing.
A: My advice is to take it slowly.

A: 궁금한 점이 있으면 주저하지 말고 전화줘.
B: 고마워, 그럴게. 이 매뉴얼은 정말 이해하기 힘든데.
A: 내 조언은 천천히 해보라는거야.

★is to~
be동사 다음에 바로 동사원형이 보어로 올 경우에는 to를 붙여 쓴다.

I-K
I
J
K

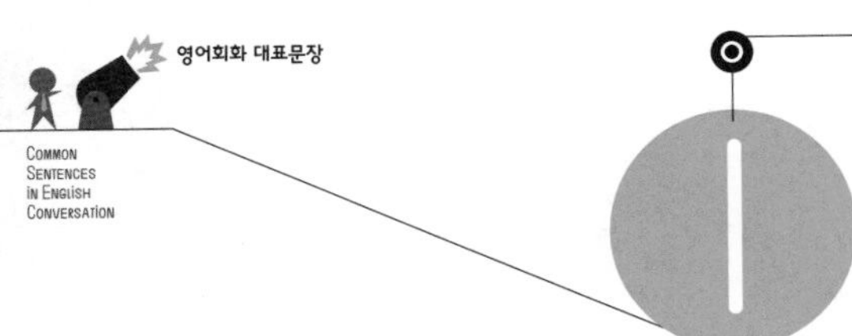

001
I (totally) forgot

(깜박) 잊었어.

거의 잊을 뻔 했지만 결국 잊지는 않했을 때는 I almost forgot!

002
I always knew you'd be successful

난 네가 성공하리라는 것을 굳게 믿었었어

003
I appreciate it

감사해요, 고마워

강조하려면 I really appreciate it(that, this).

004
I asked you to stay out of this

이거 관여하지 말라고 했잖아

"내 집에 얼씬거리지 말라고 몇 번이나 말했니?"는 How many times have I told you to stay out of my house?

005
I blew it

내가 망쳤어, 기회를 놓쳐버렸어

= I failed. blow it는 부주의나 실수로 기회를 놓치다

006 **I came by to see if you could go out for dinner with me**

나랑 저녁먹을 수 있는지 확인하러 왔어

I came by to see if~는 …인지 확인하러 왔어. I'll check to see if~ 역시 …인지 아닌지 알아보다. Let me just see if~는 …인지 확인하다

007 **I can do it**

내가 할 수 있어

"내가 할 수 있을거야. 내가 해볼게"는 I believe I can do it. Let me try

008 **I can handle it by myself**

혼자 (처리)할 수 있어

by myself는 혼자 힘으로

009 **I can see that**

알겠어, 알고 있어

= This is clear to me. I can see that S+V는 …임을 알겠다, …이구나

010 **I can't afford a lawyer**

변호사를 댈 여력이 없어

can't afford to+V[N]는 …할 여유가 없다

011 **I can't afford to buy it**

난 그걸 살 여력이 안돼

"너에게 집을 사줄 여력이 없어"는 I can't afford to buy you a house.

012 **I can't afford to hire more workers**

직원을 더 뽑을 여력이 없어

013 **I can't believe how hot it is today**

오늘 정말 무지 덥구만

I can't believe (that) S+V는 "…을 믿을 수가 없다"라는 의미로 절의 내용을 부정하는 것이 아니라 절의 내용에 놀라며 하는 말이다

014 **I can't believe it!**

설마!. 말도 안돼!

I can't believe this!는 말도 안돼!, 정말야!

015 **I can't believe it's real**

이게 사실이라는게 믿기지 않아

016 **I can't believe you did that**

네가 그랬다는 게 믿기지 않아

017 **I can't believe you never called me**

어떻게 내게 전화를 한 번도 안할 수 있어

018 **I can't do this anymore**

더 이상은 이렇게 못해

do this는 이렇게 하다

019 **I can't find it anywhere**

다 찾아봐도 없네

아무리 찾아봐도 찾을 수 없을 때

020 **I can't get there by one o'clock**

한 시까지 거기에 못 가

get there = go

021 **I can't hear you very well**

네 말이 잘 안 들려

= You weren't loud enough

022 **I can't help being cautious**

조심할 수밖에 없어

can't help ~ing = …하지 않을 수 없다 = can't help but to+V

023 **I can't help but feel a little guilty**

좀 죄의식을 느끼지 않을 수 없어

024

I can't help but think about Lisa

리자에 대해 생각하지 않을 수 없어

"널 생각하지 않을 수 없어"는 I can't help but think of you.

025

I can't seem to concentrate

집중할 수가 없는 것 같아

026

I can't take it anymore

더 이상 못견디겠어

= Something is driving me crazy

027

I can't wait for Christmas

크리스마스가 빨리 왔으면 좋겠어

"네 연설이 정말 기다려진다"는 I can't wait for your speech.

028

I can't wait for the gym to open

체육관이 빨리 열었으면 좋겠어

can't wait for ~ to+V는 어서 빨리 …가 …하기를 바라다

029

I can't wait for you to meet her

네가 걜 빨리 만났으면 좋겠어

030 **I can't wait for you to try this**

네가 이걸 했으면 좋겠어

031 **I can't wait to be with you!**

너랑 빨리 함께 있고 싶어

can't wait to+V는 주어가 어서 빨리 …하기를 바라다

032 **I can't wait to go!**

어서 가고 싶어!

033 **I can't wait to meet you**

널 몹시 만나고 싶어

034 **I can't wait to sleep with her**

걔하고 자고 싶어

sleep with = have sex with

035 **I can't wait to tell you this**

네게 이걸 빨리 말하고 싶어

036

I can't help myself

나도 어쩔 수가 없어

"나도 어쩔 수가 없었어"는 I couldn't help myself.

037

I caught a cold

감기 걸렸어

catch a cold = get a cold

038

I changed my mind

맘 바꿨어

change one's mind는 마음을 바꿔먹다

039

I couldn't care less

알게 뭐람, 전혀 상관없어

부정어+비교급 = 최상급

040

I couldn't help but wonder

의아해 하지 않을 수 없었어

041

I did it!

해냈어!

"네가 해냈어!"는 You did it!

042 **I didn't catch what you said**

네가 말한 걸 이해 못했어

"방금 말한 거 못들었는데"는 I didn't catch what you just said.

043 **I didn't come here to fight**

싸우려고 온게 아냐

I didn't come her to+V는 "난 …하러 여기에 온게 아냐"

044 **I didn't do it**

내가 그러지 않았어

"내게 뒤집어 씌우지마! 난 안 그랬어"는 Don't try to pin it on me. I didn't do it.

045 **I didn't know it was a big secret**

그게 큰 비밀인 줄 몰랐어

I didn't know S+V는 …였다는 것을 몰랐어

046 **I didn't know that you called**

네가 전화한 걸 몰랐어

047 **I didn't know that you knew that**

네가 그걸 알고 있는 줄 몰랐어

048
I didn't know that!
정말 몰랐네!

= I never heard that before

049
I didn't know we won the game
우리가 게임에 이긴 걸 몰랐어

게임에서 지다는 lose the game

050
I didn't know what else to do!
다른 무엇을 해야 할 줄 몰랐어!

"달리 어떻게 해야 할 지 모르겠어"는 I don't know what else to do.

051
I didn't know what exactly I wanted
내가 정확히 뭘 원하는 줄 몰랐어

052
I didn't know what it was
그게 무엇인지 몰랐어

053
I didn't know what to say
무슨 말을 할 줄 몰랐어

"뭐라 말해야 할지 모르겠어"는 I don't know what to say.

054 **I didn't know you needed help**

도움을 필요로 하는 줄 몰랐어

055 **I didn't know you planned a surprise birthday party**

깜짝 생일 파티를 준비할 줄 몰랐어

plan a surprise party 깜짝 파티를 준비하다

056 **I didn't know you two were dating**

너희 둘이 데이트하는 지 몰랐어

date가 동사로 쓰인 경우

057 **I didn't know you were fired**

네가 잘린 걸 몰랐어

"크리스, 꺼져, 넌 해고야!"는 Chris, get out of here. You're fired!

058 **I didn't know**

몰랐어

I didn't know (that) S+V는 "…을 몰랐어"

059 **I didn't mean it**

고의로 그런 건 아냐

= Please don't be upset by what I did or said. "고의로 그런 건 아냐. 그냥 걜 놀린 것 뿐인데"는 I didn't mean it. I was just joking with her.

060 **I didn't mean to bother you**

방해하려는 건 아니었어

I didn't mean to+V는 …하려고 그런 건 아냐

061 **I didn't mean to do that**

그럴려고 그런 게 아니었어

= Sorry for doing that

062 **I didn't mean to hurt you**

너에게 상처 줄 의도가 아니었어

"기분 나쁘라고 한 말은 아니었어"는 I didn't mean to offend you.

063 **I didn't mean to interrupt**

방해할려고 한 게 아닌데

064 **I didn't mean to say that**

그렇게 말할려는 게 아니었어

065 **I didn't order lemonade**

레모네이드 주문 안했는데요

066 **I didn't pass the exam**

시험을 통과하지 못했어

pass the exam은 시험에 통과하다. 반대로 떨어지다는 fail the exam

067 **I didn't quite get that**

무슨 말인지 전혀 모르겠네요.

여기서 get은 understand

068 **I didn't say anything**

아무 말도 안했어

"난 그렇게 말하지 않았어"는 I didn't say that

069 **I didn't say I couldn't do it**

내가 할 수 없을 거라고 말하지 않았어

I didn't say S+V난 …라고 말하지 않았어

070 **I didn't say it was funny. I said it was weird**

재미있다고 안했어. 이상하다고 말했어

I didn't say S+V. I said S+V는 난 …라고 말하지 않고 …라고 했어

071 **I didn't say that**

그렇게 말 안했어

072 **I didn't say they were married**

걔네들이 결혼했다고 말하지 않았어

073 **I didn't say you were stupid**

네가 멍청하다고 말하지 않았어

074 **I didn't sleep with your girlfriend**

네 여자친구랑 안잤어

075 **I didn't think of that**

난 그걸 생각하지 못했어

think of~는 …을 생각하다

076 **I don't believe it!**

믿을 수 없어!, 그럴리가!

I don't believe this!는 "말도 안돼!, 뭔가 이상해!" 그리고 I don't believe you!는 "뻥치지마!"

077 **I don't blame you**

그럴 만도 하지

= I'm not angry at you. 네가 화낼 만도 해는 "I don't blame you for being angry."

078 **I don't buy it**

못믿어

buy = accept or believe

079 **I don't care about that!**

난 상관안해!

"난 결과에 상관없어"는 I don't care about the result.

080 **I don't care if she's fat or thin**

난 걔가 뚱뚱하든 날씬하든 상관안해

I don't care if~ 는 …을 상관안해

081 **I don't care if you go home**

네가 집에 가도 상관없어

082 **I don't care what you think**

네 생각 관심없어

083 **I don't care who he sleeps with**

걔가 누구랑 자는지 관심없어

084 **I don't care**

상관없어

"알게 뭐람! 난 안 그만둔다고!"는 I don't care! I am not quitting!

085 **I don't feel like dancing**

춤추고 싶지 않아

I don't feel like ~ing는 …하고 싶지 않다

086 **I don't feel like doing anything**

아무 것도 하기 싫어

not doing anyting 아무것도 하지 않다

087 **I don't feel like going out today**

오늘 외출하기 싫어

go out은 외출하다

088 **I don't feel like I'm learning anything**

난 뭔가 배우고 있다는 느낌이 전혀 없어

I don't feel like S+V는 …한 것 같지 않아

089 **I don't feel like it**

그러고 싶지 않아, 사양할래

090 **I don't feel like making dinner tonight**

오늘밤 저녁하기 싫어

make dinner 저녁 준비를 하다

091 **I don't feel like shopping today**

오늘 쇼핑하기 싫어

092 **I don't feel well**

기분이 안 좋아

feel well 기분이 좋다

093 **I don't get it**

모르겠어

"이해가 안돼. 뭐가 우습다는거야?"는 I don't get it. What's so funny?

094 **I don't have a choice**

선택의 여지가 없어

강조하려면 I don't have any choice

095 **I don't have a plan**

계획이 없어

A-D E-H I-K L-P S-T U-W Y

096 **I don't have any brothers**

형제가 아무도 없어

"친구가 하나도 없어"는 I don't have any friends

097 **I don't have any money**

돈이 하나도 없어

"현금이 하나도 없어"는 I don't have any cash

098 **I don't have any questions**

아무런 질문도 없어

"뭐 질문이라도 있어?"라고 하려면 Do you have any questions for us?

099 **I don't have much time**

시간이 별로 없어

"이거 마치는데 시간이 얼마 없어"는 We don't have much time to finish this.

100 **I don't have time**

시간이 없어

"이럴 시간이 없어"는 I don't have time for this.

101 **I don't know about that**

그건 잘 모르겠어, 글쎄

상대방의 말에 살짝 반대하는 의미의 문장. = That seems incorret.

102 **I don't know anything about that**

그거에 대해 전혀 몰라

I don't know anything about ~는 "…에 대해 아무것도 몰라"

103 **I don't know how to say it in English**

이걸 영어로 뭐라고 하는 지 모르겠어

I don't know how to+V 어떻게 …하는지 몰라

104 **I don't know how to thank you**

뭐라 감사해야 할지 모르겠네요

= How can we ever thank you?

105 **I don't know if it's such a good idea**

그게 좋은 생각인지 모르겠어

I don't know if S+V는 …인지 모르겠어

106 **I don't know the exact figure**

정확한 숫자는 몰라

107 **I don't know the first thing about computers**

컴퓨터에 대해 아무 것도 몰라

= I have no knowledge of computers

108 I don't know what I'm going to do

뭘 해야 할지 모르겠어

긍정적인 대답은 Don't worry. You can try again!

109 I don't know what to do

어떻게 해야 할지 모르겠어

"어떻게 해야 할지 모르겠어. 넘 혼란스러워"는 I don't know what to do. I'm all mixed up.

110 I don't know what to say

(감사 혹은 실망하여) 뭐라 해야 할지 모르겠네요

= I can't express what I'm thinking

111 I don't know what you mean

무슨 말인지 모르겠어

= I don't understand that = I'm not sure what you mean

112 I don't know what you're talking about

(놀라거나 황당해하며) 어째서 그런 소리를 하는 거야

What are you talking about?는 그게 무슨 소리야?

113 I don't know why

왜 그런지 이유를 모르겠어

I don't see why not은 "그래"

114 **I don't know. I'm not sure of anything yet**

몰라. 아직 아무것도 몰라

be not sure of~는 …에 대해 알지 못하다

115 **I don't like doing the washing**

세탁하는 걸 싫어해

do the washing은 세탁하다(do the laundry), do dishes는 설거지하다

116 **I don't like this**

(이게) 마음에 안 들어

117 **I don't mean it**

그럴 생각은 아냐, 진심은 아냐

118 **I don't mean to cut you off**

말을 끊으려고 했던 건 아니지만

I don't mean to do~는 "…하려는 게 아니다"

119 **I don't mean to make things worse**

사태를 더 나쁘게 만들려는 것은 아니지만

make things worse 상황을 더 나쁘게 만들다

120
I don't see any problems here

여기 아무 문제도 없어

121
I don't see that

난 그렇게 생각하지 않아, 그런 것 같지 않아

122
I don't think I can do this

내가 이걸 할 수 없을 것 같아

I don't think~ 역시 자기가 말하려는 내용을 부드럽게 해주는 역할로 다만 상대방과 반대되는 의견이나 자기가 말할 내용이 부정적일 경우에 사용하면 된다.

123
I don't think I can live without you

너없이 살 수 없을 것 같아

live withou sb는 …없이 살다

124
I don't think I'm better than you

내가 너보다 낫지 않아

be better than sb는 …보다 낫다

125
I don't think it is going to happen

그럴 리는 없겠지

126 **I don't think it'll rain tomorrow**

내일 비가 올 것 같지 않아

127 **I don't think she can do it**

걔가 하지 못할 것 같아

128 **I don't think so**

그렇지 않아, 아닐 걸

= Probably not

129 **I don't think that's a good idea**

그게 좋은 생각같지 않아

여기서 that은 접속사가 아니라 지시대명사로 주어로 쓰였다.

130 **I don't think that's possible**

그럴 리가 없을 걸

131 **I don't think that's the problem**

그게 문제가 아닌 것 같아

132 **I don't think we have anything in common**

우리 공통점이 없는 것 같아

have sth in common는 …을 공통점으로 갖다

133 **I don't think we should do that**

우리가 그걸 해야 한다고 생각지 않아

134 **I don't want to be rude**

무례를 범하고 싶지 않아

I don't want to+V는 …을 하고 싶지 않다

135 **I don't want to get drunk tonight**

오늘밤 취하고 싶지 않아

get drunk는 취하다

136 **I don't want to go to work**

출근하기 싫어

go to work는 출근하다. I have to go to work는 출근해야 돼

137 **I don't want to lose you**

너를 잃고 싶지 않아

138 **I don't want to work overtime everyday**

매일 야근하고 싶지 않아

work overtime은 야근하다

139 **I don't see that happening**

그렇게는 안될걸

= I think that won't occur

140 **I don't think you have done a good job**

네가 일을 제대로 못한 것 같아

do a good job은 일을 잘하다

141 **I end up divorcing my wife**

결국 난 아내와 이혼해

end up ~ing는 결국 …하게 되다

142 **I enjoyed myself very much**

무척 즐거웠어

"해변에서 즐거웠어"는 I enjoyed myself at the seaside.

143 **I enjoyed talking with you**

너랑 얘기해서 즐거웠어

헤어질 때 하는 인사말

144
I enjoyed the party

파티 즐거웠어

"저녁 즐겁게 먹었어"는 I enjoyed the dinner.

145
I enjoyed your company

같이 있어서 즐거웠어

company는 회사가 아니라 일행, 동행이라는 뜻. 또한 I'm expecting company는 누가 오기로 되어 있어

146
I entirely agree with you

전적으로 동감이야

= I can't disagree with you = I couldn't agree with you more

147
I feel bad

기분이 안좋아

feel bad 기분이 안좋다, 속상하다

148
I feel better

기분이 나아졌어

강조하려면 I feel much better

149
I feel like an idiot

내가 바보가 된 것 같아

feel like+N은 …인 것 같아

150 **I feel like having a cup of coffee**

커피 먹고 싶어

feel like ~ing은 …하고 싶다

151 **I feel like having a drink**

술 한잔 하고 싶어

have a drink는 술 한잔하다

152 **I feel like I'm never going to find him**

절대로 걔를 못 찾을 것 같아

I feel like S+V는 …한 것 같아

153 **I feel like I've been here before**

전에 여기 와본 것 같아

have been here before는 전에 와보다

154 **I feel like it**

하고 싶어

반대는 I don't feel like it

155 **I feel like it's my fault**

내 잘못 인 것 같아

be one's fault는 …의 잘못이다

156 **I feel like my head is going to explode**

머리가 터질 것 같아

157 **I feel like taking a shower**

샤워 하고 싶어

"나 샤워중인데"는 I'm in the shower

158 **I feel much better now**

이제 기분이 더 나아졌어

159 **I feel sick**

몸이 아파

160 **I feel so stressed out today**

오늘 스트레스 엄청 받았어

"회사에서 스트레스 엄청받았어"는 I'm stressed out at work

161 **I feel so unhappy about my life right now**

지금 내 인생이 너무 우울해

feel unhappy about~은 …에 대해 만족하지 못해

162 **I feel sorry for you**

네게 미안해

163 **I feel tired**

피곤해

"조금 피곤해"는 I'm kind of tired. "너 정말 피곤해 보인다"는 You seem really tired

164 **I felt so embarrassed about it**

그 때문에 무척 당황했었어

= I'm so humiliated

165 **I find that hard to believe**

그게 믿겨지지 않아

find sth+형용사는 …을 …라고 생각하다

166 **I forget she's thirteen**

걔가 13살이라는 걸 잊었어

I forget (that) S+V는 …라는 걸 잊다

167 **I forgot about our date, I'm so sorry**

데이트하는 걸 잊었어. 미안해

I forget about+N은 …을 잊다

168 **I forgot my cell phone charger**

핸드폰 충전기를 잊고 두고 왔어

I forget sth은 …을 잊고 두고 오다

169 **I forgot to call you**

너한테 전화하는 걸 잊었어

I forget to+V는 …하는 걸 잊었어

170 **I forgot to tell you about the party**

파티에 대해 네게 얘기하는 걸 잊었어

"사장이 전화했다는 걸 깜박잊고 네게 얘기 못했어"는 I forgot to tell you that the boss called.

171 **I found it on the internet**

인터넷에서 봤어

find sth on the internet은 인터넷에서 …을 보다

172 **I get your point**

무슨 말인지 알겠어

= I see what you mean

173 **I got a new job**

새로 취직했어

"새로운 일은 어때?"는 How's it going with your new job?

174 **I got behind schedule**

예정보다 늦었어

175 **I got fat these days**

요즘 살쪘어

get fat은 뚱뚱해지다, 살찌다. "다시 살찌겠어"는 I'm going to get fat again. "살이 쪘어"는 I've put on[gained] weight

176 **I got him to turn in the report**

걔가 레포트를 제출하도록 했어

get sb to+V는 사역동사로 …가 …하도록 하다(= have sb+V)

177 **I got home after work**

퇴근 후에 집에 갔어

"오늘 저녁 퇴근 후에 전화할게"는 I'll call you after work tonight.

178 **I got it**

알았어

= I understand now. 어, 알았어. "제 시간에 갈게"는 Sure, I got it. I'll be there on time.

179 **I got it from her**

걔가 준거야

get sth from~는 …로부터 …을 받다

180 **I got it on sale**

세일 때 산 거야

get sth on sale은 세일할 때 사다

181 **I got lucky**

난 운이 좋았어

get lucky는 운이 좋다

182 **I got my car washed**

세차했어

get sth+pp는 제 3자에게 …을 …하게 하다

183 **I got the flu**

독감 걸렸어

get the flu는 독감으로 get a cold와 구분해야 한다

184 **I got the promotion**

나 승진했어

"승진에서 떨어졌어"는 I didn't get the promotion

185 **I got there on time**

제 시간에 도착했어

"시간 맞춰왔네"는 You're on time

186 **I got to ask you something**

뭐 좀 물어봐야겠어

"물어보고 싶은 게 있는데"는 I want to ask you something.

187 **I got to go see my lawyer**

가서 변호사 만나야 돼

go see = go to see

188 **I guess I should call her**

걔한테 전화해야 될 것 같아

I guess 주어+동사의 경우도 I think와 유사한 표현으로 역시 확신이 없는 이야기를 전달할 때 혹은 전달하는 이야기를 부드럽게 할 때 쓰는 표현

189 **I guess I'll see you at dinner**

저녁 때 봐요

식사명(breakfast, lunch, dinner) 앞에는 무관사

190 **I guess I'm done**

끝낸 것 같아

be done = be finished

191 **I guess I'm excited. It has been a while**

내가 신난 것 같아. 오랜간만이잖아

be excited 흥분하다, 신나하다

192 **I guess it's a little better now**

지금 좀 나아진 것 같아

193 **I guess it's time we talked about this**

이거에 대해 얘기해야 될 것 같아

It's time S+V는 당연히 해야 할 것을 하지 못하고 있다는 뉘앙스

194 **I guess it's worth a try**

한 번 해 봄직도 한데

be worth+N[~ing]은 …할 가치가 있다. be worthy of~역시 …할 가치가 있다. 전치사 of의 유무에 주의

195 **I guess we don't have a choice**

우리에게 기회가 없는 것 같아

196 **I guess we should go**

우리 가야 될 것 같아

197 **I guess you're right**

네 말이 맞는 것 같아

I guess so는 상대방의 얘기에 가볍게 동조할 때 "아마 그럴거야"라는 말

198

I had a bad day

진짜 재수없는 날이야

= This day was difficult for me. "직장에서 안좋았어?"는 Bad day at work?

199

I had a pretty hectic day

정신없는 날이었어

= I was very busy

200

I had my computer upgraded

컴퓨터를 업그레이드 했어

have sth+pp는 제 3자를 시켜 pp하게 시켰다라는 말로 get sth+pp와 같은 표현

201

I had my hair cut

나 머리 잘랐어

미장원에서 머리를 잘라주기 때문에 have sth+pp를 쓴다.

202

I had my secretary work on it

비서보고 그 일을 하라고 했어

have sb+V = get sb to+V

203

I had no idea you were from New York

네가 뉴욕 출신이라는 걸 몰랐어

I have do idea = I don't know. be from~은 …출신이다

204 **I had to break up with her**

걔랑 헤어져야만 했어

break up with sb는 …와 헤어지다

205 **I hate this as much as you**

너만큼이나 이거 싫어해

206 **I hate to disturb you, but this is important**

방해하기 싫지만 중요한 문제라서

I hate to disturb you, but~ 는 방해하기 싫지만~

207 **I hate you and that's why I'm leaving**

널 싫어해서 내가 떠나는 거야

That's why S+V는 그래서 …하다

208 **I have a call on the other line**

다른 전화가 와서

209 **I have a cold**

감기 걸렸어

have+질병 : I have a headache는 머리가 아프다

210 **I have a date tomorrow night**

내일 밤 데이트있어

211 **I have a good idea**

내게 좋은 생각이 있어

212 **I have a hard time getting up early in the morning**

아침 일찍 일어나는게 힘들어

have a hard time ~ing는 …하는데 힘들어하다

213 **I have a hunch that I'll fail the exam**

시험에 떨어질 것 같아

= I think that S+V. 여기서 hunch는 예감, 육감

214 **I have a question for you**

질문이 하나 있는데요

= Can I ask you a question?

215 **I have an appointment**

약속이 있어

"다른 약속이 있어"는 I have another appointment.

216 **I have an early class tomorrow**

내일 아침 일찍 수업이 있어

217 **I have been pretty busy**

꽤 바빴어

218 **I have been to the station**

역에 갔다 왔어

have been to+장소는 …에 갔다 왔다. 장소명사로는 bathroom, station, beauty salon이나 혹은 좀 오래 머무르는 New York 등의 단어가 올 수도 있다.

219 **I have company**

일행이 있어

= I'm busy talking with these people right now.

220 **I have feelings for her**

걔를 좋아해

have feelings for sb는 …을 좋아하다, have a feeling은 …인 것 같아

221 **I have just finished it**

방금 그걸 끝냈어.

finsh sth = have finshed sth = be finished with sth

222 **I have my notebook stolen**

노트북을 도둑맞았어

steal한 것이 제 3자인 도둑놈이기 때문에 have sth+pp

223 **I have never heard of such a thing**

그런 일은 들어본 적이 없어

= I'm not sure if it's true.

224 **I have no choice but to do that**

그러지 않을 수 없어

have no choice but to+V는 …을 하지 않을 수 없다

225 **I have no idea**

몰라

여기서 idea는 기발한 생각, 창의력이 아니다. 단순히 = I don't know

226 **I have no idea how this works**

이게 어떻게 그렇게 되는지 모르겠어

"그렇게는 안돼"는 That's not how this works

227 **I have no idea how to help you**

널 어떻게 도와야 할 지 모르겠어

228 **I have no idea what to say**

무슨 말을 해야 할지 모르겠어

= I can't express what I'm thinking = I don't know what to say

229 **I have no idea what you just said**

네가 방금 뭘 말했는지 모르겠어

230 **I have no idea what you're talking about**

네가 무슨 말을 하는 건지 모르겠어

231 **I have nothing to do with that affair**

난 그 사건과 아무런 상관이 없어, 관련이 없어

have nothing to do with~는 …와 상관[관련]이 없다

232 **I have to ask you something**

뭐 좀 물어볼 게 있어

여기서 I have to는 의무라기보다는 "내가 …을 할 수밖에 없음"을 표현

233 **I have to cancel tomorrow's meeting**

내일 회의를 취소해야 되겠어

have to = must

234 **I have to finish it by tomorrow**

내일까지는 이걸 마쳐야 돼

by tomorrow는 내일까지 딴 짓을 하더라도 결과적으로 내일까지 끝낸다는 말이고 until을 쓰면 내일까지 지속적으로 계속이라는 의미.

235 **I have to go have dinner with my son**

아들과 저녁먹으러 가야 돼

have dinner with sb는 …와 함께 저녁을 먹다

236 **I have to go there this afternoon**

오늘 오후에 거기에 가야 돼

237 **I have to make money**

돈을 벌다

make money는 돈을 벌다, make much money는 돈을 많이 벌다

238 **I have to say good bye now**

지금 헤어져야겠어

say good bye는 작별인사를 하다

239 **I have to talk to you**

얘기 좀 하자고

240

I have to tell you something

말할게 하나 있는데, 정말이지

"할 말이 있어. 네 아내에 관련된거야"는 I have to tell you something. It's about your wife.

241

I haven't decided yet

아뇨, 아직 못정했는데요

decide = make up one's mind

242

I haven't made up my mind yet

아직 결정을 못했는데

0243

I haven't seen you in ages

오랜만이야

in ages 대신에 for a long time을 써도 된다.

244

I hear you

듣고 있어

"네말 들었어"는 I heard you

245

I heard about your daughter

네 딸 얘기 들었어

hear about~는 …에 대한 얘기를 듣다

246 **I heard him yelling from behind**

난 걔가 뒤에서 소리치는 걸 들었어

hear sb ~ing는 …가 …하는 것을 듣다

247 **I heard that you failed the entrance exam**

입학시험에 떨어졌다며

I heard that S+V는 …했다며

248 **I heard that**

그거 들었어

"나도 들었어"는 I heard that too.

249 **I heard what happened to her yesterday**

어제 걔한테 무슨 일이 일어났는지 들었어

250 **I heard you were going to get married**

너 결혼할거라고 그러던데

get married 결혼하다, be married 결혼한 상태이다

251 **I hope so**

그랬으면 좋겠어

= It would be great if that happened. I hope not은 그러지 말았으면 좋겠다

A-D E-H I-K L-P S-T U-W Y

252 **I hope we will win**

우리가 이기기를 바래

I hope S+V는 …이기를 바래

253 **I hope you aren't angry**

네가 화 안내기를 바래

254 **I hope you get well soon**

곧 낫기를 바래

get well soon 곧 나아진다, 좋아지다

255 **I hope you'll come again**

네가 다시 오길 바래

256 **I hope you'll enjoy the movie**

네가 그 영화를 좋아하길 바래

257 **I hope you'll like it**

네가 그걸 좋아하길 바래

258 **I hope you're right**

네 말이 맞았으면 좋겠어

259 **I just want to apologize for that**

난 그거에 대해 사과하고 싶어

apologize for sth은 …에 대해 사과하다. 사과하는 사람을 쓰려면 apologize to sb

260 **I just wanted to let you know how much I care about you**

내가 널 얼마나 생각하는지 알려주고 싶었어

care about 신경쓰다

261 **I just wanted to let you know that I'm going to really do my best**

내가 정말 최선을 다할거라는 걸 알려주고 싶었어

262 **I just wanted to make sure you got home safe**

단지 네가 집에 무사히 왔는지 확인하고 싶었어

make sure S+V는 …을 확인하다

263 **I keep bumping into you around here**

이 근처에서 자주 만나네

bump into = come across = run around = 우연히 마주치다

264

I keep thinking about her

계속 걔 생각만 해

keep ~ing는 계속해서 …하다

265

I keep trying to get a date with Pam

팸하고 데이트하려고 계속 시도중이야

try to+V는 …하려고 시도하다

266

I knew it!

나도 안다고!, 그럴 줄 알았다니까!

= I was sure that was true

267

I know how to handle it

그걸 어떻게 처리해야 하는지 알어

handel = deal with = 다루다

268

I know how to play chess

체스 어떻게 하는 지 알아

play+무관사 운동명, play the+악기명

269

I know how you feel

네 심정 알아

= I know the feeling

270 **I know she made a mistake**

걔가 실수했다는 걸 알아

make a mistake는 실수하다

271 **I know what I'm doing**

내가 다 알아서 한다구

= I can do this well

272 **I know what it is**

그게 뭐인지 알아

273 **I know what it's like to be a teenager**

10대라는 게 어떤 건지 알아

You don't know what it's like to+V는 넌 …가 어떤건지 몰라

274 **I know what you mean**

무슨 말인지 알아

= I had a similar experience

275 **I know what you're up to**

네 속셈 다 알아

= I understand your secret motive or goal

276 **I know where to go**

어디로 가야 할 지 알아

277 **I left my cell phone on the desk when I'm getting out of the office**

퇴근할 때 책상에 핸드폰을 두고왔어 get out of the office 퇴근하다, 사무실에서 나오다

278 **I left the key in the room**

방에 열쇠를 두고 나왔어

leave sth+장소는 …에 …을 두고 나오다

279 **I like listening to classical music**

클래식음악 듣는 걸 좋아해

listen to~는 …을 듣다

280 **I like to play golf**

골프치는 걸 좋아해

like to+V[~ing]는 …하는 것을 좋아하다

281 **I like watching good movies on TV**

TV에서 좋은 영화 보는 걸 좋아해

282 **I like you the best**

네가 제일 좋아

283 **I lost my passport. What should I do?**

여권을 잃어버렸는데. 어떻게 해야죠?

lose sth은 …을 잃어버리다

284 **I made a big decision**

큰 결정을 했어

make a decision = decide

285 **I made a mistake**

내가 실수했어

큰 실수를 했을 때는 I mad a huge mitake

286 **I made it!**

쉽지 않은 일을 해냈어!

= I succeeded. You made it은 너 해냈구나. He made it big은 걘 크게 성공했어

287 **I mean business**

진심이야

= I don't mean maybe = 대충하는 말아냐. 진심이야

288 **I mean it**

진심이야

= This is true

289 **I mean, what about you?**

내 말은, 넌 어때?

I mean,은 상대방이 내가 한 말을 못알아 들었을 때 혹은 내가 이건 다시 설명을 해주어야겠다고 생각들 때 필요한 표현

290 **I mean, she's just a friend**

내 말은 걘 그냥 친구야

291 **I meant to say thank you**

미안하지만 네게 고맙다고 말할 생각이었어

I meant to say~는 …라고 말하려고 했어

292 **I missed my connecting flight to NY**

뉴욕행 연결 비행편을 놓쳤어요

293 **I must be going**

나 가야 돼

= I think I should be going = I think I'd better be going

294 **I must be off**

이제 가봐야겠어

be off는 떠나다, 출발하다. I am off는 "나 간다." I'd better be off는 "나 먼저 갈게"

295 **I must go now**

지금 가야 돼

296 **I must say good bye**

그만 헤어져야 돼

say good bye 작별인사를 하다

297 **I need more time to decide**

결정할 시간이 더 필요해

I need more time to+V는 …할 시간이 더 필요하다

298 **I need some rest**

좀 쉬어야겠어

get some rest는 좀 쉬다

299 **I need to get back to the office**

사무실로 돌아가야 돼

get back to+장소는 …로 돌아가다. get back to sb는 …에게 나중에 연락하다

300

I need to get some sleep

좀 자야겠어

"바람 좀 쐬야겠어"는 I need to get some air

301

I need to go to the bathroom right now

지금 화장실로 가야 돼

need to+V는 …해야 한다

302

I need to stay another day

하루 더 머물러야 돼

303

I need to talk to you

너하고 얘기 좀 해야겠어

304

I need you to finish this by tomorrow

내일까지 이걸 끝내야 해

I need you to+V는 네가 …를 해야 돼

305

I need you to pay attention

주목해 주세요

pay attention은 주목하다

306 **I need you to sign the document**

서류에 서명을 해줘

sign the document는 서류에 서명하다

307 **I need you work faster**

일을 더 빨리해

308 **I need your help**

네 도움이 필요해

309 **I never thought I would outlive him**

내가 걔보다 오래 살리라곤 생각못했어

I never thought I would+V 내가 …하리라고는 생각도 못했어

310 **I never thought I'd say this**

내가 이 말을 하리라곤 꿈에도 생각 못했어

311 **I never thought this would happen**

이런 일이 벌어지리라고는 생각못했어

312 **I prefer draft beer**

생맥주가 좋아

I prefer sth은 …을 더 좋아하다

313 **I prefer indoor sports to outdoor sports**

실외운동보다는 실내운동을 좋아해

prefer A to B는 B보다 A를 더 좋아하다

314 **I prefer to be alone**

혼자 있는 게 더 좋아

prefer to+V는 …하는 걸 더 좋아하다

315 **I put on weight, though I have been on a diet**

다이어트를 했는데도 살이 쪘어

put on weight = get fat, be on a diet는 다이어트를 하다

316 **I really enjoyed it**

난 정말 즐거웠어

317 **I saw him working in the office today**

오늘 그가 사무실에서 일하는 거 봤어

see sb ~ing는 …가 …하는 것을 보다

318 **I saw you with some girl last night**

네가 간밤에 어떤 여자랑 있는 걸 봤어

see sb with sb는 …가 …와 함께 있는 것을 보다

319 **I screwed up**

완전히 망쳤어

= I made a mistake. "내가 크게 망쳤어"는 I screwed up big time. "네가 일을 망쳤어"는 You screwed up

320 **I should go now**

지금 가야 돼

should는 약한 의무로 ought to

321 **I should go see what's going on**

무슨 일인지 가서 봐야겠어

go on = happen

322 **I should have told you**

네게 말했어야 하는데

should have+pp는 …을 했어야 했는데 하지 못했다라는 말

323 **I shouldn't have done it**

그렇게 해서는 안되는 거였는데

shouldn't have+pp는 반대로 …을 하지 말았어야 했는데 해버렸다는 후회의 말

324 **I shouldn't have said yes**

승낙하지 말았어야 했는데

"그렇게 말하지 말았어야 했는데"는 I shouldn't have said that

325 **I shouldn't have tied you up so long**

너무 오래 붙잡고 있었네요.

전화나 방문해서 상대방의 시간을 너무 뺐었다고 할 때

326 **I talk in my sleep**

나 잠꼬대 해

327 **I think I can do that**

할 수 있을 것 같아

328 **I think I'd better be going now**

지금 가봐야 될 것 같아

= I think I must be going now

329 **I think I'm done now**

이제 끝낸 것 같아

be done = be finished

330 **I think it's a good idea**

좋은 생각인 것 같아

반대는 I don't think it's a good idea

331 **I think it's high time to make a toast**

건배를 해야 할 것 같아

make a toast는 건배하다. 내가 축배를 할게는 I'd like to make a toast

332 **I think it's time for a change**

변화할 때인 것 같아

333 **I think it's too expensive**

너무 비싼 것 같은데요

expensive의 반대는 cheap

334 **I think it's weird**

이상한 것 같아

335 **I think we should host a housewarming party**

집들이를 해야 될 것 같아

host~는 모임 등을 주최하다

336

I think you'll enjoy it

네가 즐겨할거야

"네가 좋아할 것 같아"는 I think you'll like it.

337

I think you're right

네가 맞는 것 같아

338

I thought I told you not to come

오지 말라고 한 것 같은데

I thought I told you not to+V는 …하지 말라고 한 것 같은데

339

I thought I told you to go to bed

가서 자라고 말한 것 같은데

go to bed 자다, 잠자리에 들다

340

I thought so

(나도) 그렇게 생각했어, 그럴 것 같았어

so 대신에 too을 써도 된다.

341

I thought that I could trust him

믿을 수 있는 사람인 줄 알았는데

I thought last night was great라고 하면 "지난밤은 정말 좋았다고 생각해"라는 말이 된다. 하지만 그렇게 생각했지만 실제는 그렇지 않은 경우에도 많이 사용된다.

342 **I thought you had the day off**

하루 쉬는 지 알았어

have the day off 하루 쉬다

343 **I thought you knew it**

네가 알고 있는지 알았어

344 **I thought you liked him**

네가 걜 좋아하는 줄 알았어

345 **I thought you said it was okay**

난 네가 괜찮다고 말한 줄 알았는데

I thought you said S+V는 난 네가 …라고 말한 줄 알았는데

346 **I thought you were leaving**

네가 떠나는 줄 알았어

347 **I thought you were on my side**

난 네가 우리편인 줄 알았어

be on one's side는 …의 편이다

348 **I told you so**

내가 그랬잖아

"전에 내가 말했잖아"는 I told you before

349 **I told you he didn't do it**

걔가 그러지 않았다고 했잖아

I told you S+V는 네게 …라고 말했잖아

350 **I told you not to do that!**

그러지 말라고 했잖아!

I told you not to+V는 네게 …하지 말라고 했잖아

351 **I told you that**

내가 그랬잖아

352 **I told you to get out of here**

꺼지라고 말했잖아

"날 떠나라고 했잖아"는 I told you to leave me.

353 **I told you to give her whatever she wants**

걔가 원하는 건 다 주라고 했잖아

354 **I took her to a restaurant**

걔를 식당에 데려갔어

take sb to+장소명사는 …을 …로 데려가다

355 **I used to go to church**

교회에 가곤 했었어

used to+V는 과거의 규칙적인 습관, "매일 조깅했었어"는 I used to jog everyday. 주의할 점은 지금은 하지 않는다는 의미를 포함한다.

356 **I want to ask you something**

뭐 좀 물어볼게

I want to+V는 …을 하고 싶어 = I'd like to+V

357 **I want to get good seats**

좋은 자리에 앉고 싶어

get good seats는 좋은 자리를 차지하다

358 **I want to make sure it's perfect**

그게 완벽한지 확인하려고

I want to make sure S+V는 …을 확인하고 싶어

359 **I want to make sure that you're okay**

네가 괜찮은 지 확인하고 싶어서

360 I want to talk to you

너하고 얘기하고 싶어

"그거에 대해 너하고 얘기하고 싶어"는 I want to talk to you about that.

361 I want to thank you for helping me

도와줘서 고마워요

362 I want you out

나가

"꺼지라고"는 I want you out of here, "당장 이리와"는 I want you right here.

363 I want you to feel free to have fun while you're on vacation

휴가 때 마음편히 재미있게 보내

364 I want you to meet my friend, Sam

인사해, 내 친구 샘야

사람 소개할 때 꼭 필요한 패턴.

365 I wanted to let you know you did okay

네가 잘 했다는 걸 알려주고 싶었어

I wanted to let you know S+V는 난 네게 …을 알려주고 싶었어

366 **I was going this way anyway**

어쨌든 난 이쪽으로 가려고 했어

go this way는 이쪽 방향으로 가다

367 **I was just trying to help you**

난 그저 널 도와주려는 거였어

368 **I was just wondering why you're here**

왜 네가 여기 있는지 생각해봤어

I was just wondering why S+V 난 왜 …인지 생각해봤어

369 **I was just wondering**

그냥 궁금해서

"고향이 어디야? 그냥 궁금해서"는 What's your hometown? I was just wondering.

370 **I was on my way home from work**

퇴근해서 집에 오는 길이었어

"브라이언 집에서 돌아오는 길이었어"는 I was just on my way back from Brian's house.

371 **I was out looking for a job all day**

온종일 일자릴 구하러 다녔어

look for는 …을 찾다

372 **I was somewhere else**

잠시 딴 생각했어

= I wasn't paying attention

373 **I was stuck in traffic**

차가 막혔어

= I will be late because I can't drive quickly

374 **I was told that he's not coming**

걘 안온다고 들었어

I was told that S+V는 …라고 얘기들었어

375 **I was too embarrassed to tell you**

너무 당황스러워서 네게 말할 수 없었어

too~ to+V는 너무 …해서 …하다

376 **I was very impressed**

정말 감동받았어

"그리 나쁘지 않아. 감동받았어"는 Not bad. I'm impressed.

377 **I was watching TV**

TV를 보고 있었어

378 **I was wondering if I could ask you something**

혹 뭐 좀 물어봐도 될까요

I was wondering if ~ could~는 부탁의 문장으로 혹 …해줄래요? = Could I do this?

379 **I went back to return it**

그걸 돌려주러 갔었어

go back to+V는 …하려고 돌아가다

380 **I went back to the park**

공원으로 돌아갔어

go back to+장소는 …로 돌아가다

381 **I went on a date with this guy I met online**

온라인에서 만난 사람과 데이트했어

go on a date with sb는 …와 데이트하다

382 **I went to a Chinese restaurant for lunch**

점심먹으러 중국식당에 갔었어

I went to+장소는 …에 갔었다

383 **I went to a party last night**

어젯밤에 파티에 갔었어

A-D E-H I-K L-P S-T U-W Y

384 **I went to college**

대학교에 진학했어

"대학은 안갔어"는 I didn't go to college

385 **I went to the gas station**

주유소에 갔어

386 **I went to the mall and bought some clothes**

쇼핑몰에 가서 옷 좀 샀어

387 **I wish I could but I can't. I'm quite busy**

그러고 싶지만 안돼. 많이 바빠서

"미안. 그러고 싶지만 그럴 수가 없네"는 I'm sorry, I wish I could, but I can't do it.

388 **I wish I could help you, but I can't**

도와주고 싶지만 그럴 수가 없어

I wish I could+V는 내가 …을 할 수 있다면 좋겠어

389 **I wish I could stay longer**

더 남아 있으면 좋을 텐데

390 **I wish I had a girlfriend**

여자친구가 있었으면 좋겠어

I wish I had+N는 내게 …가 있으면 좋겠어

391 **I wish I had a lot of money**

돈이 많았으면 좋겠어

392 **I wish I had the chance to say to her**

걔에게 말할 기회가 있었으면 좋겠어

have the chance to+V …할 기회가 있다

393 **I wish I was dead**

죽었으면 좋겠어

I wish I was~는 내가 …라면 좋겠어

394 **I wish it had never happened**

그러지 않았더라면 좋았을텐데

I wish S+had+pp는 과거와 반대되는 사실을 말할 때

395 **I wish she was my wife**

걔가 내 아내라면 좋을텐데

A-D | E-H | I-K | L-P | S-T | U-W | Y

396 **I wish you a good luck**

행운을 빌어

여기서 wish는 단순히 희망하다, 바란다라는 의미

397 **I wish you could stay one extra day**

네가 하루 더 머물면 좋을 텐데

398 **I won't change my mind**

마음 바꾸지 않을게

won't = will not

399 **I won't let it happen again**

다시는 그러지 않을게

"다시는 그러지 말라"고 할 때는 Don't let it happen again.

400 **I won't tell anyone**

아무한테도 말하지 않을게

"네 아버지에게 말하지 않을게, 약속해"는 I won't tell your father. I promise.

401 **I wonder if we could get together on the 15th**

15일에 만날 수 있을까

get together 만나다, get-together 모임

402 **I wonder if you really like it**

네가 그걸 정말 좋아할 지 모르겠어

403 **I wonder what's going on**

웬일인지 모르겠어

404 **I wonder why she broke up with me**

걔가 왜 나랑 헤어졌는지 모르겠어

I wonder why S+V 왜 …인지 모르겠어

405 **I would play the violin when I was young**

어렸을 때 간혹 바이올린을 켰어

would는 과거의 불규칙적인 행위를 의미

406 **I would very much like to attend**

꼭 참석하고 싶어

I'd like to+V의 강조어법으로 very much가 삽입되었다.

407 **I'd appreciate it if you kept it secret**

네가 그걸 비밀로 해주면 고맙겠어

I'd appreciate it if you could[과거동사]는 …해주면 감사하겠습니다. 부탁의 패턴

408 **I'd be pleased if you could join us for dinner**

저녁식사를 함께 했으면 좋겠네요

I'd be pleased if you could~는 …했으면 좋겠네요

409 **I'd better get back to work**

다시 일해야겠어

I'd better = I had better+V는 난 …해야겠어

410 **I'd better get going**

출발해야겠어

get going = leave 가다, 출발하다

411 **I'd like a window seat**

창가 좌석으로 주세요

I'd like+N는 …을 달라는 말로 I want+N과 같은 의미

412 **I'd like another beer**

맥주 한잔 더 주세요

"햄과 계란 요리 주세요"는 I'd like the ham and eggs please.

413 **I'd like it medium rare**

살짝 익힌 걸로 주세요.

"고기를 적당히 익혀주세요"는 I'd like my steak medium.

414 **I'd like my coffee with milk**

커피에 우유를 타 주세요

415 **I'd like to check out now**

체크아웃하려고요

check out 확인하다, (호텔)체크아웃하다, (도서관) 책을 빌리다

416 **I'd like to get a refund on this**

이거 환불받고 싶은데요

get a refund on~는 …을 환불받다

417 **I'd like to go for a walk. Do you mind?**

산책하고 싶은데, 괜찮겠어?

go for a walk는 산책하다

418 **I'd like to propose a toast**

건배하자

propose a toast = make a toast = 건배하다

419 **I'd like to talk to you about that**

너와 그거에 대해 얘기하고 싶어

I'd liek to+V는 …하고 싶다. 좀 더 친한 사이에는 I want to+V

420 **I'd like to thank you guys for coming here**

너희들 와줘서 고마워

421 **I'd like to, but I have to go right now**

그러고 싶지만 난 지금 바로 가야 돼

I'd like to, but I have to+V는 그러고 싶지만 난 …해야돼라는 뜻으로 거절할 때

422 **I'd like you to come to my party**

네가 파티에! 왔으면 좋겠어

come to one's party는 …의 파티에 오다

423 **I'd like you to leave right now**

지금 당장 떠나줘

424 **I'd like you to meet my boyfriend**

내 남자친구하고 인사해

소개표현

425 **I'd like you to talk with her**

걔하고 얘기를 해봐

426 **I'd love to, but I have to go early tonight**

그러고 싶지만 안돼. 오늘 저녁 집에 일찍 가야 돼

I'd love to = I'd like to

427 **I'd love to, but I'm a little tired**

그러고 싶지만 안돼. 좀 피곤해서

428 **I'd rather do it myself**

내가 직접 하는 게 낫겠어

I'd rather+V는 차라리 …하는게 낫겠어

429 **I'd rather go home**

집에 가는 게 낫겠어

430 **I'd rather not say**

말 안하는 게 낫겠어

I'd rather not+V 차라리 …하지 않는게 낫겠어

431 **I'd rather not**

그러지 않는게 낫겠어

432 **I'd rather take a nap than go shopping**

쇼핑가느니 낮잠을 자겠어

take a nap은 낮잠을 자다

433 **I'd rather take a subway**

차라리 전철을 탈래

take a subway는 지하철을 타다

434 **I'd rather talk to you**

네게 이야기하는 게 낫겠어

435 **I'd really prefer to be alone**

정말 혼자 있고 싶어

I'd prefer to+V는 …하고 싶겠어

436 **I'll be back soon**

곧 돌아올게

= I'll be right back

437 **I'll be done as soon as I can**

가능한 한 빨리 끝낼게

438 **I'll be sure to do that**

반드시 그것을 할게

be sure to+V는 반드시 …하다

439 **I'll be sure to keep an eye on her**

반드시 걔를 지켜볼게

"아침에 서류 반드시 읽을게"는 I'll be sure to read the papers in the morning.

440 **I'll call you later**

나중에 전화할게

"오후 늦게 전화할게"는 I'll call you later this afternoon.

441 **I'll check if she's all right**

걔가 괜찮은지 확인해볼게

I'll check if S+V는 …인지 확인할게

442 **I'll check it out**

내가 확인해볼게

443 **I'll come over here at 12 if that's okay**

괜찮다면 내일 12시에 올게

come over는 들르다, 방문하다

444 **I'll do my best**

내 최선을 다할게

do one's best는 최선을 다하다

445 **I'll do that**

그럴게, 그렇게 할게

= I'm going to finish this job

446 **I'll do the same**

나도 똑같이 할게

447 **I'll drink to that**

찬성이야

= That sounds good to me

448 **I'll explain on the way**

가면서 설명해줄게

on the way는 이동중에, 가는 길에

449 **I'll get back to you**

나중에 알려줄게

get back to sb는 나중에 얘기하다, 나중에 전화하다

450 **I'll get him for you**

걔 바꿔줄게요

전화상 바꿔주거나 혹은 실제로 데려올 경우

451 **I'll get him to apologize to you**

걔가 너에게 사과하도록 할게

get sb to+V는 …에게 …하도록 시키다

452 **I'll get it for you**

그거 가져다줄게, 사줄게

get sth for sb는 …에게 …을 가져다주다, 사주다

453 **I'll get right on it**

바로 시작할게

= I will do it now

454 **I'll get something for you**

뭐 좀 갖다줄게

you에게 something을 가져다줄 때

455 **I'll get you a beer**

맥주 갖다줄게

"변호사 구해줄게"는 I'll get you a lawyer.

456 **I'll give her a chance**

걔에게 한번 기회주지

give sb a chance는 …에게 기회를 주다

457 **I'll give you a call**

내가 전화할게

give sb a call은 …에게 전화다

458 **I'll give you a ride**

태워다 줄게

give sb a ride는 차로 태워주다

459 **I'll go do that now**

이제 그걸 할게

go do = go to do

460 **I'll go with you next time**

다음 번에 너와 함께 갈게

461 **I'll have him call you back**

걔에게 전화하라고 할게

call sb back는 …에게 전화를 다시하다

462 **I'll have the same**

(식당에서) 같은 걸로 주세요

= I want to order that too

463 **I'll help you fix your computer**

네 컴퓨터 고치는 거 도와줄게

help sb+V는 …가 …하는 것을 도와주다

464 **I'll keep my fingers crossed**

내 행운을 빌게

keep one's fingers crossed 행운을 빌어주다. 간단히 My fingers are crossed라고 해도 된다.

465 **I'll keep my word**

내 약속할게

= I give you my word. …을 약속할게는 I give you my word S+V. 또한 "내 약속하지"는 You have my word.

466 **I'll keep that in mind**

명심할게

keep sth in mind는 가슴에 새겨두다, 명심하다

467 **I'll let you know as soon as he gets home**

걔가 집에 오면 바로 알려줄게

get home은 집에 오다

468 **I'll let you know if I can**

가능한지 알려줄게

469 **I'll let you know if it's a boy or a girl**

남자애인지 여자애인지 알려줄게

출산전에 할 수 있는 말

470 **I'll let you know later**

나중에 알려줄게

"찾으면 알려줄게"는 I'll let you know when I find it

471 **I'll let you know when I'm finished**

내가 끝마치면 알려줄게

472 **I'll let you know when the surgery is over**

수술이 끝나면 알려줄게

be over는 끝나다

473 **I'll make sure it gets done**

그 일을 확실히 끝내도록 할게

I'll make sure S+V는 …을 확실히 하다

474 **I'll make sure they know all about you**

걔네들이 너에 대한 모든 걸 알고 있도록 할게

475 **I'll pick you up on my way home**

집에 가는 길에 픽업할게

"여덟 시에 픽업할게"는 I'll pick you up at eight.

476 **I'll put you through right away**

바로 바꿔드릴게요

"그 분 바꿔드릴게요"는 I'll put you through with him.

477 **I'll see if he's in**

계신지 알아볼게요

be in는 안에 있다

478 **I'll see if she wants to come back**

걔가 돌아오고 싶어하는지 알아볼게

I'll see if S+V는 …인지 알아보다

479 **I'll show you around the office**

사무실을 구경시켜줄게

show sb around+장소는 …을 구경시켜주다

480

I'll stop by you on my way home

집에 가는 길에 네게 들를게

"여기 오는 길에 햄버거 먹었어"는 I had a burger on the way here.

481

I'll take a rain check this time

다음으로 미뤄야겠어

= Let's do it later. "오늘 바빠, 하지만 다음에 가자"는 I'm busy today, but I'll take a rain check.

482

I'll take care of it myself

내가 처리할게, 나한테 맡겨

= Let me take care of it

483

I'll take notes for you

내가 대신 노트해 줄게

484

I'll take this one

이걸로 할게

여기서 take는 선택하다, 결정하다

485

I'll take you there

널 거기에 데려갈게

take sb+장소명사[부사]는 …을 …로 데려가다

486 **I'll tell you what**

이러면 어떨까

= I'm going to give you my opinion

487 **I'll think about it**

생각해볼게

= Let me think about it = I'll give you an answer later

488 **I'll try and get there as soon as possible**

가능한 한 빨리 도착하도록 할게

as soon as possible 가능한 한

489 **I'll try to be more careful**

더 조심하도록 할게

I'll try to+V는 …하도록 할게

490 **I'll try to forget it**

잊지 않도록 할게

491 **I'll try to imporve my efforts**

더욱 노력할게

492 I'm a little confused

좀 혼란스러워

be confused = be mixed up

493 I'm all right with that

난 괜찮아

"난 괜찮아. 더 이상 사용하지도 않는데"는 I'm all right with that. I don't use them anymore.

494 I'm a stranger here too

나도 초행길이어서요

= I'm a stranger here myself

495 I'm afraid I can't

미안하지만 안돼

496 I'm afraid I don't know what to say

뭐라고 해야 할지 모르겠어요

I'm afraid S+V는 …한 것 같아 = I'm sorry to tell you this, but S+V

497 I'm afraid I've got some bad news

안 좋은 소식이 좀 있어

have got some bad news는 좀 안좋은 소식이 있다

498 **I'm afraid she's right**

미안하지만 그 여자의 말이 맞는데요

499 **I'm afraid so**

안타깝게도 그런 것 같아

= I regert that it's true.

500 **I'm afraid to be alone at night**

밤에 혼자 있는게 무서워

I'm afraid to+V는 …하는게 두려워

501 **I'm afraid we already have plans**

우린 이미 약속이 있어

502 **I'm afraid we can't do anything**

우리가 아무 것도 할 수 없을 것 같아

503 **I'm afraid you're wrong**

네가 틀린 것 같아

be wrong는 틀리다

504 **I'm afraid you've got a breast cancer**

유방암이신 것 같아요

"암으로 죽다"는 die of cancer

505 **I'm against the plan. It seems like a bad idea**

난 그 계획에 절대 반대야. 안 좋은 생각같아

be against~는 …에 반대하다, 찬성하다는 be for~

506 **I'm all ears**

귀 쫑긋 세우고 들을게

= be ready and eager to listen

507 **I'm almost through with the docs**

서류 정리 거의 다 끝나가요

be through with~는 …을 끝내다, doc = document

508 **I'm ashamed of you**

너 때문에 부끄러웠어

= I think your behavior was bad, "넌 스스로 부끄러운 줄 알아라"는 You should be ashamed of yourself.

509 **I'm aware of that**

나 그거 알고 있어

be aware of~는 …을 알고 있다

510 **I'm aware of what I owe**

내가 무슨 신세를 지고 있는지 알아

owe는 신세지다, 빚지다

511 **I'm being helped now**

다른 사람이 봐주고 있어요

512 **I'm calling to ask you for a favor**

도움 좀 청하려고 전화했어

I'm calling to+V는 …하려고 전화했어

513 **I'm calling to make an appointment with Dr. Laura**

로라선생님 예약하려고 전화했는데요

make an appointment with~는 …에게 예약하다

514 **I'm dead serious**

진짜야

여기서 dead는 강조어구

515 **I'm done with it**

난 그거 끝냈어

= I'm through with it. "내가 선택을 마쳤어. 이것들이 최종적인거야"는 I'm done with my choices. These are final.

516 **I'm done with this marriage**

난 결혼생활 끝냈어

517 **I'm for it**

난 찬성이야

반대는 I'm against it

518 **I'm getting better these days**

요즘 좀 나아지고 있어

be getting better는 점점 더 나아지고 있다

519 **I'm getting used to it**

적응하고 있어

get[be] used to sth은 …에 적응하다

210 **I'm glad to hear that**

그 얘기를 들으니 기쁘네

I'm glad to hear~는 …을 들으니 기뻐

521 **I'm glad to hear you say that**

네가 그렇게 말해줘서 기뻐

522 **I'm glad to help you**

널 도와주어서 기뻐

523 **I'm glad to meet you**

널 만나서 기뻐

524 **I'm glad to see you're doing okay**

네가 잘 지낸다니 좋아

"네가 괜찮다니 기뻐"는 I'm glad to see you're okay.

525 **I'm glad to see you're so concerned about me**

네가 내 걱정을 해준다니 기뻐

526 **I'm glad you came here**

네가 여기 와줘서 고마워

"네가 여기 있어 얼마나 기쁜지 몰라"는 I'm so glad you're here.

527 **I'm glad you decided to stay**

네가 남아있기로 해서 고마워

I'm glad S+V는 …해서 기뻐

528 **I'm glad you enjoyed it**

네가 즐겼다니 기뻐

529 **I'm glad you feel that way**

그렇게 생각한다니 기뻐

feel that way는 그렇게 생각하다

530 **I'm glad you like it**

네가 좋아하니 나도 좋아

531 **I'm glad you think so**

그렇게 생각해줘 기뻐

532 **I'm going shopping today**

오늘 나 쇼핑하러 간다

"다음 주에 낚시하러 가"는 I'm going fishing next weekend.

533 **I'm going to visit her in New York this spring**

이번 봄에 뉴욕에 있는 걔를 방문할거야

534 **I'm going to be a little late**

나 좀 늦을거야

다음에 할 말은 I'll try and get there as soon as possible.

535 **I'm going to bed**

나 자러간다

go to bed는 침대로 가는게 아니라 그냥 자다라고 생각하면 된다.

536 **I'm going to Florida for a couple weeks**

몇 주 정도 프랑스에 가 있을려구

be going to+장소는 …에 갈거야

537 **I'm going to go do the laundry**

세탁하러 가야겠어

be going to+V는 …할거야, 여기서 going에는 '가다'라는 의미는 없다.

538 **I'm going to go take a bath**

가서 목욕 좀 할거야

take a bath는 목욕하다, 샤워하다는 take a shower

539 **I'm going to go to Yale some day**

언젠가 예일대에 들어갈거야

some day는 at some time in the future

540 **I'm going to Japan for a week on business**

사업상 일주일간 일본에 갈거야

on business는 사업차

541 **I'm going to leave for Canada**

캐나다로 떠날거야

leave+장소명사는 …을 떠나다, leave for+장소명사는 …로 향해 출발하다

542 **I'm going to quit this job**

난 이 일을 그만둘거야

quit this job은 이 일을 그만두다

543 **I'm going to study English**

영어공부할거야

544 **I'm going to take some time off**

좀 쉴거야

take some time off는 좀 쉬다

545 **I'm going to the bathroom now**

지금 화장실 좀 갔다올게

546 **I'm going to the library**

나 도서관에 가

547 **I'm going to the same direction**

같은 방향으로 가

go to the same direction은 같은 방향으로 가다

548 **I'm going to the store**

가게에 갔다올게

549 **I'm gonna take off**

나 갈게

take off = leave

550 **I'm happy for you**

네가 잘 돼서 기뻐

"내가 도움이 돼서 정말 기뻐. 네가 잘돼 기뻐"는 I'm so glad I could help. I'm happy for you.

551 **I'm happy with that**

난 그거에 만족해

be happy about[with]는 …에 만족하다

552

I'm having fun

재미있어

have fun은 즐거운 시간을 보내다, have much fun은 아주 즐거운 시간을 보내다

553

I'm here to pick up Jane

제인 데리러 왔어요

I came here to~라고 해도 된다.

554

I'm here to complain about the noise

시끄럽다고 항의하러 왔는데요

complain about[of]~는 …을 항의하다

555

I'm in charge of it

내가 그 책임자야

be in charge of~는 …을 책임지다

556

I'm just here to say I am sorry

미안하다고 말하려고 왔어

557

I'm just looking around

그냥 둘러보는 거예요

"그냥 구경하고 있는거예요"는 I'm just looking.

558 **I'm just so excited about having her here**

걔가 여기 온다는게 너무 기대돼

be excited about~ing는 …하는거에 신나하다

559 **I'm just trying to focus on this**

이거에 집중하려고 하고 있는거야

be trying to+V는 …하려고 하다

560 **I'm kind of embarrassed**

난 좀 당황스러워

kind of = sort of = 좀, 약간

561 **I'm like you**

나도 너랑 같은 생각이야

여기서 like는 전치사

562 **I'm listening**

말해봐, 어서 말해

= I'm waiting to hear what you say. "내말 듣고 있는거야?"는 Are you listening to me?

563 **I'm looking forward to hearing from you soon**

곧 소식듣기를 바랍니다

"곧 너를 만나보고 싶어"는 I'm looking forward to seeing you soon. "토요일 밤이 기다려져"는 I'm really looking forward to Saturday night.

564 **I'm looking forward to it**

그게 몹시 기다려져

to~다음에는 ~ing만 오는게 아니라 명사가 오기도 한다.

565 **I'm looking forward to working with you**

너랑 함께 무척 일하고 싶어

566 **I'm lost**

길을 잃었어

be lost = get lost는 길을 잃다

567 **I'm mad at you**

너한테 화가 나

= get angry with

568 **I'm not allowed to have coffee**

난 커피마시면 안돼

be not allowed to+V는 …해서는 안되다

569 **I'm not familiar with this area**

여기 지역은 잘 모르는데요

= I'm a stranger here, too

570 **I'm not feeling well**

기분이 별로 안좋아

571 **I'm not going**

난 안가

반대로 (모임 등에) 간다고 갈 때는 I'm going. 이는 그냥 간다(I'm leaving)는 의미로는 쓰인다.

572 **I'm not good at presentation**

난 발표회에 익숙하지 않아

be good at~는 …에 익숙하다, 잘하다. 반대는 be not good at 혹은 be terrible at

573 **I'm not good at this**

난 이거에 능숙하지 못해

574 **I'm not happy with my job**

내 일에 만족을 못하겠어

be not happy with~는 …에 만족하지 못하다, 불만이다

575 **I'm not here to get you in trouble**

널 곤란하게 하려고 여기 온 게 아냐

get in trouble은 곤경에 처하다, get sb in trouble은 …을 곤경에 처하게 하다

576 **I'm not in the mood**

그럴 기분이 아냐

= I don't want to do it now

577 **I'm not interested in playing golf**

골프치는데 관심없어

be interested in+N[~ing]는 …하는데 관심있다

578 **I'm not lying**

거짓말 아니야

= I'm being honest

579 **I'm not ready**

준비 안됐어

be ready for+N[to+V]는 …할 준비가 되어 있다

580 **I'm not so sure that's a good idea**

그게 좋은 생각인지 잘 모르겠어

I'm not so sure S+V는 …인지 잘 모르겠다

581 **I'm not supposed to be here**

난 여기 있으면 안돼

= It's wrong to be here.

582 **I'm not supposed to do that**

난 그러면 안돼

I'm not supposed to+V는 …하면 안돼. be supposed to + V …하기로 되어 있다.

583 **I'm not sure**

잘 모르겠어

"그건 확실히 몰라"는 I'm not sure about that.

584 **I'm not sure if he's done with it yet**

걔가 그걸 마쳤는지 모르겠어

I'm not sure if S+V는 …인지 잘 모르겠어

585 **I'm not sure if I am available Friday**

내가 토요일에 시간되는지 모르겠어

be available는 시간이 되다

586 **I'm not sure if I can do that**

내가 그걸 할 수 있을런지 모르겠어

587 **I'm not sure if she's going to marry me**

걔가 나하고 결혼할런지 모르겠어

marry sb는 …와 결혼하다. marry to[with] sb로 쓰면 안된다.

588 **I'm not sure what you mean**

무슨 말인지 모르겠어

"…를 말할 때 그게 무슨 말이야"는 I'm not sure what you mean when you say ~

589 **I'm not sure where to go**

어디로 가야할 지 모르겠어

590 **I'm off**

오늘 비번야

= I'm done working for today. be off duty 비번이다, be on duty 근무중이다

591 **I'm on it**

내가 할게

= I'll try to do it

592 **I'm on my way**

지금 가고 있는 중이야

"나 집[체육관]에 가는 길이야"는 I'm on my way home[to the gym].

593 **I'm out of luck**

난 운이 없어

= I don't have a chance to do something.

594 **I'm pissed off**

열받아

= I'm very angry

595 **I'm planning to buy a new car**

차를 새로 뽑으려고

be planning to+V[on ~ing]는 …할 생각이야

596 **I'm proud of you**

네가 자랑스러워

be proud of sb는 …을 자랑스러워하다

597 **I'm ready to go now**

지금 갈 준비됐어

"그거 할 준비됐어"는 I'm ready to do it

598 **I'm really going to miss you**

보고 싶을거야

= I wish you wouldn't go away.

599 **I'm really happy that you called me**

전화해줘서 정말 기뻐

be happy that S+V는 …해서 기쁘다

600
I'm really tired after working all day

온 종일 일하고 나니 정말 피곤해

after working all day는 온 종일 일하고 나니

601
I'm serious

정말야

"진심이야 크리스. 짐쌌고 나 떠나"는 I'm serious. Chris. I packed my things and I'm leaving

602
I'm sick of this

난 이게 지겨워

= This is tiring or boring me.

603
I'm so into you

난 걔한테 빠져있어

be into sb는 …에 빠지다, be into sth은 …에 열중하다. 그래서 "난 그런거 안해"는 I'm not into it.

604
I'm so exhausted

난 지쳤어

"너 지쳐 보여. 어떻게 된거야?"는 You look exhausted. What's the story?

605
I'm so humiliated

창피해 죽겠어

= I feel embarrassed about something.

606 **I'm so tired**

정말 피곤해

be tired[sick] of+N[~ing]는 …가 짜증나, 진절머리나

607 **I'm so upset that you forgot our anniversary**

우리 기념일을 잊다니 너무 화가 나

be upset that S+V는 …해서 화가 나다

608 **I'm sorry about his behavior**

걔가 그렇게 행동해서 미안해

be sorry about~는 …로 해서 미안해

609 **I'm sorry about that**

그거 미안해

610 **I'm sorry he's on the other line right now**

미안하지만 다른 전화받고 계신데요

be on the other line은 다른 전화를 받고 있다

611 **I'm sorry I can't make it**

미안하지만 못 갈 것 같아

make it (to)는 어떤 장소에 (성공적으로) 가다

612 **I'm sorry I can't talk long**

미안하지만 길게 얘긴 못해

talk long은 길게 얘기하다

613 **I'm sorry I'm late again**

또 늦어서 미안해

614 **I'm sorry I've taken so much of your time**

시간을 너무 많이 뺏어서 죄송해요

615 **I'm sorry to bother you**

귀찮게 해서 미안해

"그게 짜증나?"는 Does it bother?, "귀찮게 하려는 것은 아녔어"는 I didn't mean to bother you.

616 **I'm sorry to have kept you waiting for so long**

오래 기다리게 해서 미안

keep sb waiting for so long …을 오래 기다리게 하다

617 **I'm sorry to hear that**

안됐어

= That's too bad

618 **I'm sorry, but I can't help you**

미안하지만 도와줄 수가 없어

미안한 행동이나 말을 하기에 앞서 혹은 거절할 때는 I'm sorry, but S+V

619 **I'm sorry, but I can't speak English very well**

미안하지만 영어가 서툴러요

620 **I'm sorry, but I don't know who you are**

미안하지만 네가 누구인지 몰라

621 **I'm sorry, but I don't think so**

미안하지만 난 그렇게 생각안해

622 **I'm sorry, but I don't trust you guys**

미안하지만 너희들 믿지 않아

623 **I'm sorry, but I'm going to be a little late**

미안, 좀 늦을 것 같아

624 **I'm sorry, but I've wasted your time**

미안하지만 네 시간을 많이 뺐었네

625 **I'm sorry, but it's true**

미안하지만 사실이야

626 **I'm sorry, but the answer is no**

미안하지만 대답은 노야

627 **I'm sorry?**

예?

I'm sorry? = Excuse me? = Come again? = Pardon me?

628 **I'm sure I can do it**

내가 그걸 확실히 할 수 있어

"내가 문을 닫은 게 확실해"는 I'm sure I locked the door.

629 **I'm sure of that**

확실해

I'm sure about that이라고 해도 된다.

630 **I'm sure she's going to be all right**

재는 괜찮아 질거라고 확신해

be going to be all right 괜찮아 질거다

631 **I'm sure that won't be necessary**

그게 꼭 필요하지 않을 수도 있을거야

won't = will not

632 **I'm talking to you**

내가 하는 말 좀 잘 들어

= I want you to listen to me

633 **I'm telling you**

정말야, 잘 들어

= Believe what I say

634 **I'm the one who quit the job**

회사 그만 둔 사람은 나야

be the one who~ …가 …했어

635 **I'm thinking about asking her out tonight**

오늘밤 걔한테 데이트신청할까 해

be thinking about ~ing는 …할 생각이야

636 **I'm thinking about getting married**

결혼할거야

637 **I'm thinking about going to France next month**

다음 달에 프랑스에 가려고

638 **I'm thinking about taking her to a restaurant tonight**

오늘 밤에 걜 식당에 데려가려고

take sb to+장소는 …을 …로 데려가다

639 **I'm thinking I have to tell him**

걔에게 말해야 될 것 같아

I'm thinking S+V는 …할 것 같아

640 **I'm thinking I should go visit him**

걔를 방문해야 될 것 같아

go vist = go to visit

641 **I'm thinking of going on vacation**

휴가갈까 생각중야

be thinking of ~ing = be thinking about ~ing

642 **I'm thinking of inviting Betty**

베티를 초대할까봐

643 **I'm thinking of quitting soon**

곧 그만둘까 생각중야

644 **I'm tied up with my work all day long**

온종일 일때문에 꼼짝달싹하지 못했어

be tied up with~는 …에 꼼짝달싹하지 못하다

645 **I'm with you**

동감이예요

"그 말에 공감해"는 I'm with you there. "내 의견에 동의해?"는 Are you with me on this?

646 **I'm working for him**

걔 밑에서 일해

work for sb는 …의 밑에서 일하다, …에서 일하다

647 **I'm working on it**

지금 하고 있어

= I'm trying to complet it

A-D E-H I-K L-P S-T U-W Y

648 **I'm working out on Sundays**

난 일요일마다 운동해

work out은 특히 짐(gym)에서 하는 운동을 말한다.

649 **I'm worried**

걱정돼

650 **I'm worried about my career**

내 경력이 걱정이 돼

be worried about sb[sth]는 …을 걱정하다

651 **I'm worried about my reputation**

내 명성이 걱정이 돼

652 **I'm worried about that**

그게 걱정이 돼

653 **I'm worried about you**

네가 걱정돼

654 **I'm worried about your health**

네 건강이 걱정돼

655 **I'm worried I might be late**

늦을까봐 걱정돼

be worried S+V는 …을 걱정하다

656 **I'm worried that it's too late**

너무 늦었을까봐 걱정돼

657 **I'm worried you might be a little cold**

네가 좀 춥지 않을까 걱정돼

658 **I've been dying to go there**

거기 정말 가고 싶어했어

be dying to = be eager to = can't wiat to~

659 **I've been in India for two weeks**

2주간 인도에 갔었어

I've been in+장소는 …에 있었어, …에 갔다 왔어

660 **I've been in the lab all day**

하루 종일 실험실에 있었어

661 **I've been there**

무슨 말인지 충분히 알겠어, 정말 그 심정 이해해 본 적 있어

662 **I've been to this place before**

전에 여기에 와봤어

663 **I've decided to break up with him**

나 걔랑 헤어지기로 결정했어

생각 끝에 결정하는 거라 decide의 경우 현재완료 형으로 자주 쓰인다.

664 **I've decided to stay more**

더 머물기로 결정했어

665 **I've got a date**

데이트가 있어

"오늘 저녁 줄리와 데이트가 있어"는 I've got a date with Julie this evening.

666 **I've got a new plan now**

이제 새로운 계획이 있어

have = have got, 단 have가 …을 갖고 있다라는 의미에 한함.

667 **I've got a question**

질문이 있어

668 **I've got so much to do**

할 일이 너무 많아

669 **I've got something for you**

네게 줄게 있어

670 **I've got something in my eye**

눈에 뭐가 들어갔어

671 **I've got to go do this thing**

이 일을 해야겠어

have got to+V = have to+V

672 **I've got to go now**

나 이제 가야 돼

673 **I've got to go to see the dentist**

나 치과에 가야 돼

674 **I've had enough of you**

네가 지겨워

= I don't want to see you anymore

675 **I've had it**

질렸어, 이제 그만

= I'm going to do something to change this

676 **I've heard so much about you**

너에 대해 많은 얘기 들었어

677 **I've never been there**

거기 가본 적이 없어

"전에 거기에 가본 적이 없어"는 I've never been there before.

678 **I've never been to a bachelor party before**

전에 총각파티에 가본 적이 없어

have been to~는 …에 가본 적이 있다

679 **I've never been to New York**

뉴욕에 가본 적이 없어

680 **I've never really thought about it**

정말 그걸 생각해 본 적이 전혀 없어

"…에 대해 생각해봤어?"는 Have you thought about~?

681 **I've never seen anything like that**

저런 거 본 적이 없어

"정말 굉장하네. 저런 건 처음 봐"는 That's really something. I've never seen anything like it.

682 **If I had Cindy's number, I would call her**

신디 전화번호가 있으면 전화할텐데

현재와 반대되는 이야기를 가정할 때는 If 주어+과거동사, 주어+would/could+V를 쓰면 된다. 의미는 "…라면 …했을텐데"라는 의미.

683 **If I were you, I would not go**

너라면 난 가지 않을 텐데

If I were you는 내가 너라면, 역시 현재와 반대되는 가정을 하는 경우

684 **If I were you, I wouldn't let him know until tomorrow**

내가 너라면, 내일까지 걔한테 말하지 않을텐데

685 **If it's okay with you I'll take tomorrow off instead of Monday**

괜찮다면 월요일 대신 내일 쉬었으면 해 If it's okay with you는 네가 괜찮다면

686 **If there's anything else you need, you just let me know**

뭐 다른 필요한 게 있으면 알려줘

687 **If you ask me**

내 생각엔

= I'm going to give my opinion

688 **If you have any questions, give me a call**

혹 물어볼 거 있으면 전화하고

"뭐 궁금한 게 있으면 주저말고 전화해"는 If you have any questions, please don't hesitate to call me.

689 **If you need any help, you let me know**

도움이 필요하면 내게 알려줘

"뭐라도 듣게 되면 내게 알려줘"는 If you hear anything, let me know. "우리가 뭐 좀 들으면 내가 바로 알려줄게"는 If we hear anything, I will let you know right away.

690 **If you need anything, don't hesitate to ask**

필요한 거 있으면 바로 말해

don't hesitate to+V는 주저말고 …하다

691 **If you're hurry, you'll not be later for the school**

서두르면 학교에 안늦을거야

be late for~는 …에 늦다

692 **Is Andy in right now?**

앤디 지금 있나요?

Is Andy available?이라고 해도 된다.

693 **Is it all right if I ask you one more question?**

하나 더 물어봐도 돼?

Is it all right if S+V?는 …해도 괜찮아?

694 **Is it all right if I stay in New York for a few more days?**

뉴욕에 며칠 더 머물러도 될까?

695 **Is it far from here?**

여기서 멀어요?

"여기서 그리 멀지 않아요"는 It's not far from here.

696 **Is it necessary to go on a strike?**

파업을 하는 게 필요해?

go on a strike는 파업하다. go on a+명사의 형태(go on a date)

697 **Is it oaky to talk to you about this?**

네게 이거 이야기해도 돼?

Is it okay to+V?는 …해도 돼?

698 **Is it okay if I finish the apple juice?**

사과주스 마저 다 마셔도 될까?

Is it okay if S+V?는 …해도 돼?

699 **Is it okay if I go out with your sister?**

네 여동생과 데이트해도 괜찮아?

go out with sb = go on a date with sb

700 **Is it okay if I leave this stuff here**

이 물건 여기에 놔둬도 돼?

leave sth+장소는 …을 장소에 두다

701 **Is it okay if I park here?**

여기에 주차해도 돼?

702 **Is it okay to come in?**

들어가도 돼?

703 **Is it okay?**

괜찮아?

704 **Is it possible that I have a cancer?**

내가 암일 수도 있나요?

Is it possible that S+V?는 어떤 가능성을 물어보는 표현으로 …할 가능성이 있느냐는 의미

705 **Is it possible that she's coming back?**

걔가 돌아올까요?

come back은 돌아오다

706 **Is it possible you just didn't see her?**

네가 걜 보지 못했을 수도 있어?

707 **Is it safe to walk the street at night?**

밤에 거리를 걷는게 안전해?

Is it safe to+V?는 …하는게 안전해?

708
Is it supposed to snow tonight?

오늘 밤에 눈이 온대?

be supposed to+V는 …하기로 되어 있다

709
Is Jim supposed to be coming back this afternoon?

짐이 오늘 오후에 돌아오는거야?

710
Is that a yes or no?

예스야 노야?

"설명필요없어. 가부만 결정해줘"는 I don't need you to explain, I'm just looking for a yes or a no.

711
Is that clear?

분명히 알겠어?

= Did you understand what I said?

712
Is that for here or to go?

여기서 드시겠어요, 아니면 가져 가시겠습니까?

= Will you eat the food here or do you want it put in a bag so you can take it home to eat?

713
Is that possible?

그게 가능해?

"어떻게 그럴 수가 있어?"는 How is that possible?

714 **Is that so hard to believe?**

그게 그렇게 믿겨지지 않아?

hard to believe는 믿기 어려운

715 **Is that what she said?**

그게 바로 걔가 말한거야?

That's what she said는 그게 바로 걔가 말한거야

716 **Is that what you want to hear?**

그게 바로 네가 듣고 싶어하는거야?

717 **Is that what you want?**

그게 네가 바라는거냐?

718 **Is that what you're saying?**

그게 네가 말하는거야?

= Do you mean this?

719 **Is that what you're thinking?**

그게 네가 생각하는거야?

720

Is there any chance that we can get a room for the night?

하룻밤 묵을 방을 구할 수 있을까?

"이 친구를 기억할 가능성이 있어요?"는 Is there any chance that you remember this guy?

721

Is there anything else?

더 필요한 게 있으십니까?

"음료수를 더 달라"고 할 때는 Yes, could we order some more drinks please?

722

Is there anything I can do for you?

뭐 도와줄 것 없어?

"뭐 도와줄 일 없어?"는 Is there anything I can do to help?

723

Is there anything I can do to make you feel better?

너 기분좋아지게 하는데 내가 뭐 할일 없겠어?

"내가 …하는데 도움될 일 없어?"는 Is there anything I can do to do ~?

724

Is there anything I can help you?

내가 뭐 도와줄 일 있어?

Is there anything S+V?는 …해줄게 있어?

725

Is there something wrong with that?

그거 뭐 잘못된거 있어?

"너 뭐 잘못된거 있어"는 Is there something wrong with you?

726 **Is there something you need?**

네가 필요로 하는게 있어?

Is there something S+V?는 …하는게 있어?

727 **Is there something you want to say to me?**

네가 내게 말하고 싶은게 있어?

728 **Is this really necessary?**

정말 꼭 필요해?

729 **Is this seat taken?**

이 자리 임자있어요?

730 **Is this some kind of joke?**

장난하는거지?

= This can't be real = You must be joking

731 **Is this what you wanted?**

네가 원했던 게 바로 이거야?

This is what S+V의 의문형

732 **Is this what you were talking about?**

네가 말하던 게 바로 이거야?

talk about 얘기나누다, 말하다

733 **Is this what you're looking for?**

네가 찾는 게 바로 이거야?

look for는 찾다

734 **Is this your first time to do that?**

이거 처음 해보는거야?

Is this your first time to+V?는 이거 처음으로 ….해보는거야?

735 **Is this your first time you're seeing Michael?**

마이클 처음 보는거야?

Is this your first time S+V? 너 이거 처음으로 …하는거야?

736 **Is this yours?**

네꺼야?

737 **Isn't it amazing?**

멋있지 않아?

= That's great

738 **Isn't it the same in America?**

미국하고 같은거 아냐?

be the same in~는 …와 같다

739 **It could have been worse**

그나마 다행이야

더 나빠질 수도 있었다라는 말로 그나마 다행이라는 말

740 **It could have happened to anyone**

누구한테나 일어날 수 있는 일인 걸

741 **It doesn't matter anyway**

어쨌든 난 상관없어

matter는 중요하다, 관련있다

742 **It doesn't matter to me**

난 상관없어

matter to sb는 …에게 중요하다, 관련있다

743 **It doesn't matter what other people think**

다른 사람이 어떻게 생각하든 상관없어

It doesn't matter~는 …는 상관없어

744
It doesn't matter what you say

네가 뭐라고 하든 상관없어

745
It doesn't work

제대로 안돼, 그렇겐 안돼

= Something went wrong. "효과가 없을거야"는 It won't work. "그렇게는 안통해"는 It doesn't work that way.

746
It doesn't hurt to try

한번 해본다고 나쁠 건 없지

"물어본다고 나쁠 건 없지"는 It doesn't hurt to ask

747
It doesn't mean anything to me

난 상관없어

= That doesn't involve my life.

748
It has been 10 years since we were married

결혼한지 10년됐어

과거의 어떤 행위를 한 지가 얼마나 됐는지 현재완료를 써서 It has been+기간+since S+V(과거) 형태로 쓴다.

749
It has been a long day

기나긴 하루였어

It's been+시간명사로 쓰면 "…한 시간이 됐어[지났어]"라는 표현이 된다.

750 **It isn't worth the trouble**

괜히 번거롭기만 할거야

"굳이 그럴 필요까진 없어"는 It's not worth the effort

751 **It it's okay with you, I'll come to your office tomorrow**

괜찮다면 내일 사무실에 들를게

말을 하거나 듣는 사람이 있는 곳으로 이동하는 경우에는 come을 쓰고 그 외의 장소로 움직이는 경우에는 go를 쓴다.

752 **It looks good on you**

너한테 잘 어울린다

= It suits you very well

753 **It looks like fun**

재미 있는 것 같아

754 **It looks like her**

그 여자 같아.

755 **It looks like I'm going to be here all night**

밤새 내가 여기 있을 것 같아

It seems (like) that~과 같은 의미로 역시 뭔가 단정적으로 말하지 않고 조심스럽게 말하기 위한 장치

756 **It looks like it's going to rain**

비가 올 것 같아

757 **It looks like it's working!**

효과가 있는 것 같군!

work는 효과가 있다

758 **It looks like she already told you all about me**

걔가 나에 관한 모든 걸 이미 말한 것 같군

tell sb all about sb는 …에게 …에 관한 모든 것을 말하다

759 **It looks like she lied to me**

걔가 내게 거짓말한 것 같아

lie to sb는 …에게 거짓말하다. "내게 거짓말마"는 Don't lie to me

760 **It looks like she's going to break up with Tom**

걔는 탐과 헤어질 것 같아

break up with는 헤어지다

761 **It looks like we're stuck with traffic**

차가 밀리는 것 같아

be stuck with traffic은 차가 막히다

762 **It makes no difference to me**

난 상관없어

make no difference to sb는 …에게는 상관없어

763 **It makes sense**

일리가 있군

= I understand why that is true. "말도 안돼"는 That doesn't make any sense. "그게 말이 돼냐?"는 Does that make any sense?

764 **It may be worth a try**

한번 해봄직 할거야

be worth a try는 한번 해볼 가치가 있다

765 **It might be true**

사실일 수도 있어

might be~는 무늬만 과거일 뿐 의미는 …일 수도 있어, …할지도 모르겠어라는 말

766 **It must've been terrible**

끔찍했겠구만

must have+pp는 …했음에 틀림없다라는 표현

767 **It seems he has left**

걔가 떠난 것 같아

It seesm S+V는 "…하는 것 같아"라는 의미

768 **It seems like all of a sudden**

갑자기 인 것 같아

It seems 다음에 to me나 혹은 like를 삽입해서 사용해도 된다.

769 **It seems like it's time to break up with**

이제 그만 만나야 될 것 같아

770 **It seems like yesterday**

어제인 것 같아

771 **It seems that I have lost my wallet**

지갑을 잃어버린 것 같아

lose one's wallet는 지갑을 잃어버리다

772 **It seems that we got lost**

길을 잃은 것 같아

get lost = be lost

773 **It seems to me that you can't control yourself at all**

네가 너 자신을 전혀 통제 못하고 있는 것 같아

control oneself는 스스로를 통제하다, 자제하다

774 **It seems to me the client can't pay**

난 그 고객이 돈 낼 능력이 없어 보여

775 **It should be cloudy tomorrow**

내일 흐릴거야

should be~는 어떤 일이 일어나거나 혹은 어떤 사실이 맞을 거라는 추측의 의미로 사용된다.

776 **It slipped my mind**

깜빡 잊었어

slip one's mind는 깜빡 잊다 = I forgot it

777 **It sounds familiar**

익숙한 건대

778 **It sounds good to me**

좋아

779 **It takes 5 minutes to get there**

거기 가는데 5분 걸려

"여기서 거기 가는데 한 시간 걸려"는 It takes an hour from here to get there.

780 **It takes courage to do so**

그렇게 하는데 용기가 필요해

take courage[balls] to+V는 …하는데 용기가 필요하다

781 **It takes time to find the files you want**

네가 원하는 파일을 찾는데 시간이 걸려

782 **It took a long time for me to find it. I hope you like it**

찾는데 시간 많이 걸렸어. 맘에 들기 바래.

783 **It took me a long time to plan it out**

그거 짜는데 시간 많이 걸렸어

It takes me+시간+to+V는 내가 …하는데 …라는 시간이 걸리다

784 **It was a long day**

힘든 하루였어

It has been a long day라고도 한다. = Today was more difficult than usual

785 **It was fun having you**

같이 있어서 즐거웠어

We enjoyed your company와 같은 문장이지만 더 친근한 표현이다.

786 **It was nothing**

(감사하다고 할 때) 별일 아냐, 아무 것도 아냐

"별것도 아닌데. 도와주고 싶었어"는 It was nothing. I wanted to help you out.

787 **It was the first time I felt that way about her**

걔한테 그렇게 느끼는 건 처음이었어

feel that way about sb는 …한테 그렇게 느끼다

788 **It will help solve the traffic problems**

교통문제를 해결하는 데 도움이 될거야

help+V는 …하는데 도움이 되다

789 **It won't be easy for us**

우리에게 쉽지는 않을거야

790 **It won't work**

효과가 없을거야

"내 열쇠가 말을 안 들어"는 My key won't work.

791 **It works for me**

난 괜찮아

"괜찮겠어"는 Does that work for you? 단 sb works for sb는 …에서 일하다

792 **It would be nice if we could take a vacation**

우리가 휴가를 얻는다면 좋을텐데

"…하면 멋질거야"는 It'll be nice to~, "…하면 얼마나 좋을까 그냥 생각해봤어"는 I just thought it'd be nice if S+V

793 **It's a long story**

말하자면 길어

= It is complicated or hard to explain

794 **It's a possibility**

그럴 수도 있지

795 **It's a private matter**

그건 개인적인 문제야

private matter 사적인 문제

796 **It's against the law**

그건 위법이야

be against the law는 법에 위반되다

797 **It's all right with me**

난 괜찮아

798 **It's because I trust you**

그건 내가 널 믿어서지

It's because S+V는 …하기 때문이야

799 **It's been 2 years. I'm over him**

2년이 지났어. 난 걔를 잊었어

be over sb는 …을 잊다

800 **It's been 3 months since we had dinner**

우리 저녁 먹은지 3달이 지났네

801 **It's been a really long time since I've felt like this**

이렇게 느껴 본 거 정말 오랜만이야

feel like this는 이렇게 느끼다

802 **It's been a while**

오랜 만이야

It's = It has

803 **It's been a while since we talked**

우리가 얘기한 지가 꽤 됐어

804 **It's been eight days since I took a shower**

내가 샤워한 지가 8일이 지났어

805 **It's easier said than done**

말이야 쉽지

그냥 Easier said than done이라고 해도 된다.

806 **It's easy to get nervous on dates**

데이트날 떨리기 십상이지

get nervous는 초조해하다

807 **It's easy to spend more than you have**

자기 분수이상으로 소비하는 건 쉬워

808 **It's getting better**

점점 나아지고 있어

반대는 It's getting worse

809 **It's going to be all right**

괜찮을거야

all right 대신에 okay를 써도 된다.

810 **It's going to cost me a lot**

내가 돈이 많이 들거야

cost sb a lot은 …에게 많은 비용이 들게 하다

811 **It's going to happen**

그렇게 될거야

812 **It's going to take a while**

시간이 좀 걸릴거야

take a while은 시간이 좀 걸리다

813 **It's going to work**

잘 돌아갈거야

814 **It's good to hear from you again!**

네 목소리를 다시 듣게 되다니!

815 **hear from**

sb는 …로부터 소식을 듣다

816

It's hard to believe he's gone

개가 가버렸다는게 믿겨지지 않아

"걔가 죽었다는 게 믿어지지 않아"는 It's hard to believe that he's dead.

817

It's hard to believe that was six years ago

그게 6년전 일이라는게 믿겨지지 않아

It's hard to believe S+V는 …가 믿겨지지 않아 = I can't believe S+V

818

It's hard to believe

믿기지 않아

"결정하기 어려워"는 It's hard to decide.

819

It's hard to explain

설명하기 어려워

"잊어버리기 힘드네!"는 It's hard to forget!

820

It's hard to say for sure

확실히 뭐라 말하기가 힘드네요

821

It's high time we took a vacation and enjoyed ourselves

휴가를 얻어 즐길 때가 되었다

high를 씀으로써 It's time S+V의 늦었음을 강조한다.

822 **It's impossible to find the solution**

해결책을 찾을 수가 없어

"걔 아파트를 찾는 건 불가능해"는 It's impossible to find her apartment!

823 **It's just for fun**

그냥 재미로

824 **It's just hard to believe that happened to us**

그런 일이 우리에게 일어났다니 믿기지 않아

825 **It's like every day is our anniversary**

매일매일 우리 기념일 같아

like는 …와 같은이라는 의미로 It's like~하면 …와 같은 거네, …하는 것 같아, …하는 것과 같은 셈야 등의 뜻

826 **It's like it's raining!**

비가 오는 것 같아!

827 **It's like something's changed**

뭔가 바뀐 것 같아

828 **It's like you don't believe it**

넌 그걸 못믿는 것 같아

"넌 날 안 믿는 것 같아"는 It's like you don't believe me.

829 **It's much easier than you think**

네가 생각하는 거보다 훨씬 쉬워

비교급을 강조하는 것은 much

830 **It's not like it's a secret**

그게 비밀 같은 건 아냐

831 **It's not like that**

그런 거 아냐

832 **It's not that bad**

괜찮은데

= It's okay

833 **It's not the first time he talked to me**

걔가 내게 말한 건 처음이 아니야

834 **It's not your fault**

네 잘못이 아냐

"모두 다 내 잘못이야"는 This is all my fault.

835 **It's on me**

내가 낼게

be on the house는 가게가 쏘는 것을 말한다.

836 **It's on the tip of my tongue**

혀 끝에서 뱅뱅 도는데

= I forgot what it was but I will remember soon

837 **It's so complicated**

좀 복잡해

838 **It's so funny**

정말 재밌다

839 **It's the same with me**

나도 그래

840 **It's time for me to go home**

나 집에 갈 시간야

It's time for sb to+V는 …가 …할 시간이야

841 **It's time for you to make a choice**

네가 선택할 시간야

make a choice = choose

842 **It's time to go**

(집에) 가야 할 시간야

843 **It's time to go to bed**

자러 가야 갈 시간야

844 **It's time to say good-bye**

이제 헤어질 시간야

845 **It's up to you**

네가 결정할 일이야

be up to~에는 …하는 중이다라는 뜻도 있다.

846 **It's very kind of you to say so**

그렇게 말해줘서 고마워

"정말 친절하네요"는 That's very kind of you

847 **It's your turn**

네 차례야

"네가 …할 차례야"는 It's your turn to+V, "누구 차례야?"는 Whose turn is it?, "차례를 기다려"는 Wait your turn.

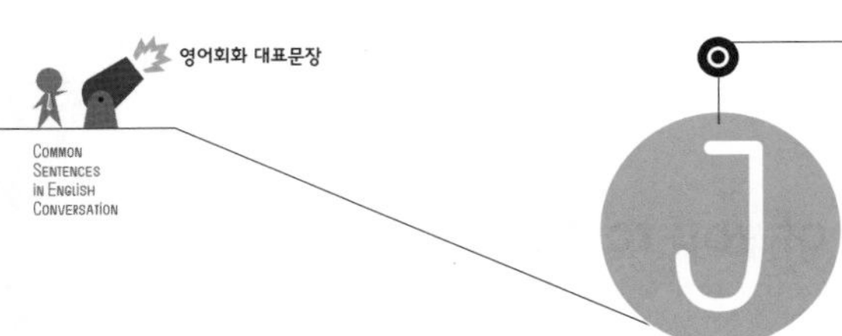

001 **Just a moment and I'll get you the manager**

잠깐만요, 매니저불러드리죠

"잠깐만요. 확인해볼게요"는 Just a moment. Let me check.

002 **Just be careful**

조심해

003 **Just call me by my first name**

이름으로 불러

call sb by sb's first name은 성이 아니라 이름으로 부르다라는 말. "우리는 이름을 부르는 사이다" 즉 친한 사이다라고 하려면 We're on a first name basis라 한다.

004 **Just don't do it again**

다시는 그러지마

005 **Just keep on trying**

계속 노력해봐

keep ~ing = keep on ~ing는 계속 …하다

006 **Just let me know if you need a hand!**

필요하면 말해!

let me know if S+V는 …인지 알려줘

007 **Just like that**

그냥 그렇게, 그렇게 순순히

= It happened quickly

008 **Just my luck**

내가 그렇지 뭐, 내가 무슨 운이 있겠어

= I always have bad luck. 앞에 That's~가 생략된 경우이다.

009 **Just tell me how you feel**

기분이 어떤지 말해봐

Can you tell me how you feel?이라고 해도 된다.

010 **Just try to enjoy yourself**

즐겁게 지내도록 해봐

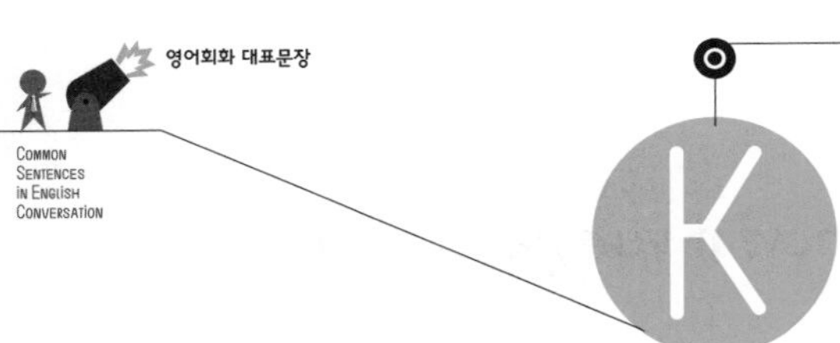

001 **Keep going**

계속 해

"교차로에 다다를 때까지 계속 가세요"는 Keep going until you come to the crossroads.

002 **Keep it up**

계속 열심히 해

= You should continue doing it that way

003 **Keep up the good work**

계속 열심히해

= Great, continue doing that

004 **Keep the change**

잔돈은 가지세요

"100 달러지폐를 잔돈으로 바꿔줄 수 있어?"를 break를 써서 Can you break a hundred?라고 한다.

005 **Keep your mouth shut**

누구한테도 말하지마

"…에 대해 입을 다물어라"는 keep your mouth shut about sb[sth]

CHECK IT OUT! 문장속에서 확인해보기!

A: Excuse me, can you tell me where the bathroom is?
B: Sure, it's just down the hall to your left.
A: Thanks, **I'll be back soon.**

A: 죄송하지만 화장실이 어디 있나요?
B: 네, 복도를 내려가다 보면 왼편에 있어요.
A: 고마워요. 곧 돌아올게요.

★Sure
앞서 언급했던 표현으로 상대의 부탁이나 제안을 듣고 「알았어」, 「그럴게」라고 답하려면, All right, Okay, Of course, Sure, No problem, Why not? 등이 있다.

A: Why are you so angry at me?
B: Because you said I was fat and ugly!
A: I didn't mean it. I was just kidding.

A: 왜 그렇게 나한테 화를 내는 거죠?
B: 나보고 뚱뚱하고 못생겼다면서요!
A: 진심이 아니었어요. 그냥 농담이었다구요.

★angry at sb
angry 대신에 mad를 써서 mad at sb 라고 해도 된다.

A: Honey, why don't we just call the plumber? I get nervous when you mess around with the pipes.
B: I know what I'm doing.
A: Somehow I doubt that.

A: 자기야, 그냥 배관공을 부르는 게 어때? 파이프를 섣불리 건드릴까봐 걱정돼.
B: 나두 다 아니까 걱정마.
A: 어쩐지 미심쩍어서 말야.

★mess around with
mess around with 잘 알지 못하면서 「…을 섣불리 다루다」(deal with something you do not understand)라는 뜻이 있다.

A: Have you heard about what happened the other day to Tara?

B: I'm all ears.

A: She got caught by the police and is going to jail.

A: 요전 날 태러한테 무슨 일이 있었는지 들었니?
B: 귀 쫑긋 세우고 들을테니까 말해봐.
A: 경찰한테 붙잡혔는데 감옥에 갈거래.

★got caught
get caught은 「잡히다」, 「체포되다」라는 의미.

A: I can't wait to get out of here.

B: I know what you mean.

A: It's so hot, and I am exhausted.

A: 여기서 나가고 싶어 죽겠어.
B: 무슨 말인지 알아.
A: 여긴 너무 덥고, 난 지쳤다구.

★exhausted
I feel very tired하다는 의미.

A: Well, **I must be off.** Got to make dinner for the kids.

B: What are you making tonight?

A: Spaghetti. My son's favorite. He's got a huge appetite!

A: 이제 그만 가봐야 돼. 애들 저녁을 만들어 줘야 하거든.
B: 오늘밤엔 뭘 만들어 줄거지?
A: 스파게티. 우리 아들이 제일 좋아하는 거거든. 걘 정말 먹성이 좋아!

★Got to
I have got to+V에서 I have가 생략된 경우.

L-P
L M N O P

L

001 **Leave it to me**

내게 맡겨

= Trust me, I'll do that

002 **Let it go**

그냥 잊어버려, 그냥 놔둬

= Try to forget it. Let it go. "그냥 잊어버려. 실수였잖아"는 It was just a mistake.

003 **Let me ask you a question**

하나 물어볼게

상대방에게 뭔가 물어볼 때 먼저 꺼내는 말. 비슷한 표현으로 Can I ask you a question?가 있다.

004 **Let me ask you something**

뭐 좀 물어볼게

= Can I ask you something?

005 **Let me check the schedule**

일정 좀 알아볼게요

"혈압 좀 재볼게요"는 Let me check your blood pressure.

006 **Let me check**

확인해볼게

Let me+V의 형태로 내가 …을 하도록 허락해달란 뜻. 어떤 행동을 하기에 앞서 상대방에게 자신의 행동을 미리 알려주는 표현법이라고 할 수 있다. 내가 …할게 정도로 해석하면 된다.

007 **Let me do it**

내가 그거 할게

008 **Let me do this for you**

널 위해 내가 이거 해줄게

009 **Let me double check**

내가 확실히 확인할게

Let's double check = Let's look at that a second time

010 **Let me explain**

내가 설명할게

011 **Let me explain why I did it**

내가 왜 그랬는지 설명할게

012

Let me get this straight

이건 분명히 해두자구

= I want to be certain I understand. "정리해보자고, 걔를 모른다는거야?"는 Let me get this straight. You didn't know him?

013

Let me get this

내가 계산할게 , 내가 맡을게

I got this라고 해도 된다.

014

Let me give you a hand

내가 도와줄게

give sb a hand는 …을 도와주다

015

Let me give you a ride home

집에까지 태워다 줄게

give sb a ride home은 집까지 차로 태워다 주다

016

Let me guess

추측해보건대, 말 안해도 알아

= I think I know the answer

017

Let me help you with your baggage

네 짐 들어주는거 도와줄게

help sb with sth는 …가 …하는 것을 도와주다

018 **Let me just see if I got this straight**

내가 제대로 이해했는지 확인해볼게요

Let me see if S+V는 …인지 확인해볼게

018 **Let me know how it goes**

그게 어떻게 돼가는지 알려줘

"어떻게 되어가는지 좀 보자고"는 We'll see how it goes.

020 **Let me know how to do it**

그걸 어떻게 하는지 알려줘

"그걸 하는 방법을 내게 묻지마"는 Don't ask me how to do it.

021 **Let me know if she likes it, okay?**

쟤가 그걸 좋아하는지 아닌지 알려줘, 응?

022 **Let me know if you have any questions**

궁금한게 있으면 알려줘

023 **Let me know what you think**

네 생각이 어떤지 알려줘

"걔네가 무슨 말을 하는지 알려줘"는 Let me know what they say.

A-D E-H I-K L-P S-T U-W Y

024

Let me know when she gets here

걔가 언제 여기에 도착하는지 알려줘

get here = come

025

Let me know where you go

네가 어디 가는지 알려줘

026

Let me make sure that I don't have any meetings

아무 회의도 없는지 확인해볼게

= Let me make sure that there's no meeting tomorrow

027

Let me make sure

하나 확실히 확인해볼게

make sure은 …을 확인하다, 확실히 하다라는 의미로 특히 Let me make sure that S+V의 형태로 자신 없는 부분을 재차 확인할 때 긴요하게 써먹을 수 있다.

028

Let me pour that for you

내가 따라줄게

pour sth는 …을 따라주다

029

Let me remind you

알려줄게 있어

= Remember that~~ "…을 명심해라"는 Let me remind you of[that]~

030 **Let me see if I understand this**

내가 이해했는지 정리해볼게요

Let me see if S+V는 …인지 알아보다

031 **Let me show you around**

구경시켜줄게요

show sb around 구경시켜주다

032 **Let me take a look at it**

그거 한번 볼게

"넌 한번 봐야 돼"는 You have to take a look at it, "(이것 좀) 봐봐"는 Take a look (at this), Please take a look at it!

033 **Let me talk to her**

걔에게 말해볼게

034 **Let me (just) say**

말하자면

= I'm going to say something quickly

035 **Let me tell you my story**

내 이야기 해줄게

"내가 다시 시작할게"는 Let me start again

036

Let me tell you something

한마디 하자면

= I'm going to tell you what I think

037

Let me think about it

생각 좀 해 보고

= I'll give you an answer later

038

Let me try again

내가 다시 해볼게

039

Let's call it a day

퇴근합시다

"오늘 일은 그만하는 게 어때?"는 What do you say we call it a day?

040

Let's do it quickly and finish as soon as possible

빨리 그걸 해서 가능한 한 빨리 끝내자

041

Let's do that

그렇게 하자

"좋아! 정말 좋겠다! 그렇게 하자!"는 That's great! That would be great! Let's do that!

042 **Let's get down to business**

일을 시작하자

Let's get serious about this = Let's get started working

043 **Let's get going**

가자고

"서둘러 가봐야겠어"는 I should get going. "늦었네. 그만 가봐야겠어"는 It's very late. We should get going.

044 **Let's get started**

자 시작하자

= Let's begin. get started (on sth)는 …을 시작하다

045 **Let's get this done first**

이거 먼저 끝내자고

get st done은 …을 끝내다

046 **Let's get together again soon**

다시 한번 보자

"조만간 한번 보자"는 Let's get together sometime.

047 **Let's go out tonight, shall we?**

오늘 밤 나가 놀자, 그럴래?

048 **Let's keep in touch!**

연락하고 지내자!

keep in touch는 서로 연락을 취하고 있다, get in touch는 연락을 하다

049 **Let's make it around four**

4시쯤 보기로 하자

= We'll meet at four

050 **Let's not think about it**

그건 생각하지 말자

Let's not+V는 …하지 말자

051 **Let's roll**

시작합시다

= Let's get started

052 **Let's split the bill**

각자 내자

split the bill은 각자 더치페이하다

053 **Let's take a break**

쉬자

take a break는 잠시 쉬다

054 **Let's talk later**

나중에 이야기하자

055 **Like this?**

이렇게 하면 돼?

= Is this right?

056 **Like what?**

예를 들면?, 어떻게?

= How can it be done?

057 **Listen to me**

내말 들어봐

"기다려. 끊지마. 내 말 좀 들어봐"는 Wait. Don't hang up. Just listen to me

058 **Long time no see**

오랫만이야

059 **Look at you!**

얘 좀 봐라!(감탄이나 비난할 때)

= You seem special or impressive. "얘 좀 봐! 이 옷 입으니 너 정말 예뻐 보여"는 Look at you! That dress makes you look so pretty.

001

Make it two

같은 걸로 주세요

= I'll get the same thing = I'll have the same

002

Make sure we don't lose it again

우리가 다시는 지지 않도록 해

상대방에게 …을 확실히 하라, …을 꼭 확인해라고 할 때는 (Please) Make sure that S+V라 하면 된다

003

Make yourself a drink and relax

술한잔 따라 마시며 편히 쉬어

004

Make yourself at home

집처럼 편히 해, 편하게 있어

= Relax and enjoy yourself there

005

Make yourself comfortable

편히 계세요

006 **May I come in?**

들어가도 되겠습니까?

007 **May I have a receipt, please?**

영수증 주실래요?

008 **May I have a word with you?**

잠깐 얘기할 수 있을까요?

have a word with sb는 …와 얘기를 나누다, have words with sb는 …와 다투다

009 **May I help you?**

뭘 도와드릴까요?

특히 상점 등에서 쓰는 전형적인 표현으로 도와드릴까요?라는 친절한 표현

010 **May I leave a message?**

메시지를 남길까요?

반대로 메시지를 남기실래요?는 May I take a message?

011 **May I see your passport[ticket]?**

여권[표]을 보여줄래요?

012

May I try it on?

입어봐도 될까요?

try sth on은 입어보다, 신어보다

013

Maybe I should call you back

다시 전화드려야겠네요

call sb back은 다시 전화하다, 회신전화를 하다

014

Maybe next time

나중에 하자

약속이나 모임 등 뭔가 행위를 다음에 하자고 미룰 때

015

Me neither

나도 그렇게 생각해, 나도 안그래

"나도 그래. 하지만 가야지 안 그러면 사장이 열받을거야"는 Me neither. But we need to go or our boss will be angry.

016

Mind your own business!

상관 말라구!

= Go away because this has nothing to do with you

017

My friends are the most important thing in my life

내 인생에서 친구가 가장 중요해

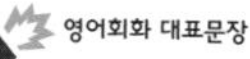

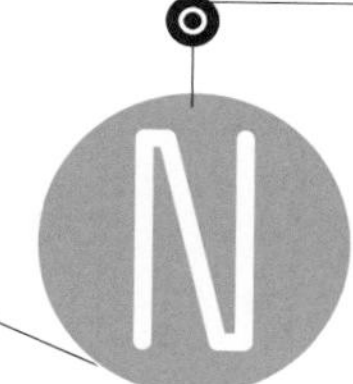

001

Never mind

걱정마, 신경쓰지마

= Forget what I asked you

002

Never say die

약한 소리하지마

003

Nice going!

잘한다!, 잘해!

= Good job! 문맥에 따라서 비아냥거릴 때도

004

Nice try!

(비록 목적달성을 하지 못했지만) 잘했어!, 잘 한거야!

"네가 지다니 안됐네. 하지만 잘했어"는 It's too bad you lost the contest. Nice try.

005

No big deal

별일 아냐

= It's not so important. "서두르지마, 별일 아냐"는 Take your time. It's no big deal.

006

No damage

손해본 거 없어

= Everything is okay. "손해본거 없고 다 괜찮아"는 No damage. Everything turned out alright.

007

No harm done

손해본 건 없어, 괜찮아

008

No offense

기분 나빠 하지마

= I didn't mean to insult you. 대답은 None taken(오해하지 않았어)

009

No problem

괜찮아, 뭘, 문제없어

= It's okay

010

No wonder

당연하지

No wonder S+V = I'm not surprised S+V

011

Not again!

또야!

= I wish this would stop happening

012 **Not always**

늘 그런 건 아냐

"꼭 그런 건 아냐"는 Not exactly

013 **Not really**

사실은 안 그래

014 **Not right now, thanks**

지금은 됐어

015 **Not so bad**

그렇게 나쁘지 않아

016 **Not that I know of**

내가 알기로는 그렇지 않아

= I don't think so

017 **Not too much**

별일 없어

"그럭저럭. 내 인생이 좀 지루해"는 Not too much. My life is kind of boring.

018 Not very much

별로 그렇지 않아

"별로 그렇지 않아. 많이 재미있게 보낸 것은 아냐"는 Not very much. It's not like we did a lot of fun things.

019 Nothing for me, thanks

고맙지만 난 됐어

권하는 음식 등을 거절하며

020 Nothing is gonna happen

아무 일도 없을거야

021 Now you go do your best

이제 가서 최선을 다해

go do = go to[and] do

022 Now you're talking!

그래 바로 그거야, 그렇지!

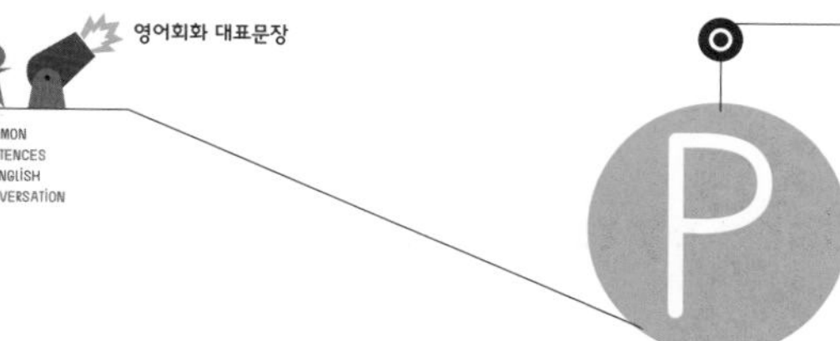

001

Please accept my sincere apologies

내 사과를 받아주라

= Will you accept my apology? 사과를 받아줄 때는 Your apology is accepted.

002

Please allow me to take your coat, sir

손님, 저에게 코트를 주시지요.

003

Please don't forget to email me

잊지말고 이멜 보내

"오늘 내 친구들 아무도 내게 이멜을 안 보냈어"는 None of my friends e-mailed me today.

004

Please excuse me for being late

늦어서 미안해

excuse sb for ~ing는 …가 …을 해서 미안하다

005

Please forgive me

제발 용서해줘

Please don't think about the bad thing I did any more.

006 **Please get it done by tomorrow**

내일 오전까지 그거 끝내

get it[this] done는 …을 끝내다

007 **Please leave me alone for a while**

잠시 날 좀 내버려 둬

leave sb alone은 …을 가만히 두다

008 **Please let me know what you'll be back**

언제 돌아오는지 알려줘

009 **Please look over the contract before you sign it**

사인하기 전에 계약서를 검토해봐

look over = examine

010 **Please tell me what happened to you**

네게 무슨 일이 일어났는지 말해줘

CHECK IT OUT! 문장속에서 확인해보기!

A: Please don't forget to make a backup of those files.
B: I'm in the process of doing so right now.
A: And leave a copy of the disk on my desk.

A: 그 화일들의 복사본을 꼭 만들어 놓으세요.
B: 지금 그렇게 하고 있는 중이에요.
A: 그러면 제 책상 위에 복사본을 놔 주세요.

★leave
「leave sth+장소」의 표현으로 「…을 …에 남겨 두다」라는 의미. 여기서는 장소로 on my desk가 쓰였다.

A: Well, it was nice talking to you.
B: You too. **Let's get together again soon.**
A: Sounds good. See you later.

A: 저기, 말씀 나누게 되서 반가웠어요.
B: 당신과 말씀 나눠 저도 반가워요. 곧 다시 만납시다.
A: 좋아요. 나중에 봅시다

★You too
It was nice talking to you, too를 줄인 표현

A: Some of us are going out for lunch, would you like to join us?
B: I am sorry I can't. I have another appointment.
A: That's fine. **Maybe next time**, okay?

A: 우리 몇 명이서 점심먹으러 나가는데, 같이 갈래요?
B: 미안하지만 못 가겠어요. 다른 약속이 있어서요.
A: 뭘요. 다음에 하죠, 네?

★Some of us
우리들 중 몇몇이라는 뜻으로 읽을 때는 「썸오브어스」가 아니라 「써머버스」라고 후다닥 발음한다.

A: May I speak to Carl, please?
B: I'm sorry, Carl just stepped out of the office. May I ask who is calling?
A: It's me, Jack.

A: 칼 좀 부탁드립니다.
B: 어쩌죠. 칼이 방금 사무실에서 나갔는데. 누구십니까?
A: 저 잭입니다.

★stepped out of the office
step out of the office는 「사무실에서 나갔다」는 말로 방금 나갔다는 걸 강조하기 위해 just와 함께 자주 쓰인다.

A: Is Jessy in the office today?
B: He is, but he is in a meeting right now.
A: May I leave a message?

A: 제시 오늘 사무실에 있나요?
B: 네, 근데 지금은 회의중이신데요.
A: 메시지를 남겨도 될까요?

★Is Jessy in~?
그냥 단순히 Is sb in?이라고 해도 된다.

A: Can I help you with anything?
B: No, thank you, I'm just looking around.
A: **Let me know** if you have any questions.

A: 도와드릴까요?
B: 고맙지만 괜찮아요. 그냥 구경만 하는 거예요.
A: 물어 보고 싶은 게 있으시면 알려 주세요.

★help you with
help의 경우, help~V, help~with, 그리고 help ~ing 등 세가지 패턴을 알아두면 된다.

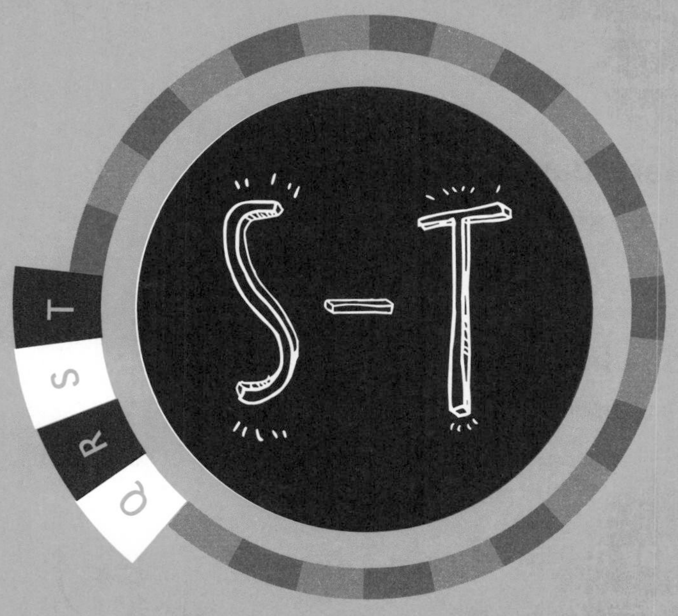
S-T
Q
R
S
T

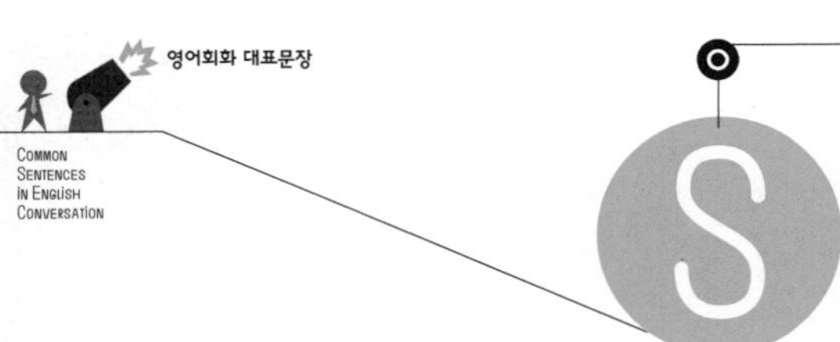

001 **Same here**

나도 그래

= I have a similar opinion

002 **Saturday would be fine**

토요일이면 좋지

003 **Say hello to your parents for me**

부모님께 내 안부 전해줘

"네 아내에게 내 안부 전해줘"는 Say hello to your wife for me.

004 **Say it again?**

뭐라고?

= What did you say? = Can you say that again?

005 **Say it once more**

한번 더 얘기해줘

006
Say when

됐으면 그만이라고 말해

= Tell me when to stop pouring your drink.

007
See you

잘 가

I'll~이 생략된 경우

008
See you around

또 보자, 이따 보자

= I will meet you again someday soon.

009
See you at 7

7시에 보자

특정시간에 보자고 할 때는 See you at+시간

010
See you back at the office

사무실에서 다시 보자

"내일 사무실에서 보자"는 (I'll) See you tomorrow at the office.

011
See you in the morning

내일 아침에 봐

012 **See you later**

다음에 보자

013 **See you soon**

곧 보자

014 **See you then**

그때 봐

약속시간이나 날짜를 잡고난 후에 하는 인사말

015 **Shall I call a taxi for you?**

택시 불러줄까요?

Shall I+V? = Let me~ = …해줄까요?

016 **Shall I give you a hand?**

도와줄까요?

give sb a hand는 도와주다

017 **Shall we eat something after work?**

퇴근 후에 뭐 좀 먹을까?

Shall we+V? = Let's+V = …하자

018 **Shall we go now?**

지금 가자

019 **Shall we go out for lunch?**

점심먹으러 나갈까?

020 **Shall we go to the movies tonight?**

오늘 밤에 영화보러 갈까?

go to the movies는 영화보러 가다

021 **Shame on you!**

부끄러운 줄 알아!

= Your actions were bad!

022 **She can't afford to lose this much blood**

이 환자는 이 정도 혈액을 잃으면 안돼요

can't afford to+V는 …할 여력이 없다

023 **She graduated from university in the State**

갠 미국대학을 졸업했어

graduate from+대학은 …을 졸업하다

024 She has worked here for 3 years

갠 여기서 일한 지 3년 됐어요

She worked here for 3 years는 지금은 여기서 일하는지 여부가 문장에 포함되어 있지 않다.

025 She is doing research on the internet

갠 인터넷 검색을 하고 있어

do research on the Internet 인터넷 검색을 하다

026 She is not my type

갠 내 타입이 아냐

"잘 생겼지만, 내 타입이 아냐"는 Good-looking, just not my type.

027 She kept on calling me

갠 계속 내게 전화를 해댔어

keep (on) ~ing는 계속해서 …하다

028 She looks like a professional

선수같아

look like+N는 …처럼 보이다

029 She might have a boyfriend

갠 남자친구가 있을지 몰라

might는 과거가 아니라 추측의 조동사

030 **She really makes me angry**

걔는 날 정말 열받게 해

make sb angry는 …을 화나게 하다

031 **She said she didn't love him**

재는 걔를 사랑하지 않았다고 했어

She said S+V는 걘 …라고 말했어

032 **She said yes**

걔가 그렇다고 했어

033 **She seems to enjoy it**

걘 즐기는 듯 보여

seem to+V는 …하는 것처럼 보여

034 **She should be home now**

걔는 지금쯤 집에 와 있을거야

shoud be~는 추측

035 **She told me she was 25**

걔는 자기가 25살이라고 했어

She told me S+V는 걘 …라고 내게 말했어

036 **She told me to tell you to call her**

걔가 너보고 자기한테 전화하라고 했어

She told me to+V는 걘 내게 …하라고 말했어

037 **She was just trying to make you feel better**

걘 널 기분좋게 해주려는 거였어

be trying to+V는 …하려고 하다

038 **She was very eager to get home**

걘 정말 집에 가고 싶어했어

be eager to = be dying to = can't wait to

039 **She went to the bathroom**

걘 화장실에 갔어

040 **She's been in New York for 8 years**

걔는 뉴욕에 8년째 살아

041 **She's chatting someone on the internet**

걘 인터넷으로 채팅중이야

chat sb on the Internet 인터넷으로 …와 채팅하다

042 **She's doing it better than me**

걔가 나보다 잘해

better than~ 는 …보다 더 잘

043 **She's gorgeous**

걘 멋져

goegeous는 멋진

044 **She's talking on the phone**

걔 지금 전화하고 있어

talk on the phone은 통화중이다

045 **She's very supportive**

걘 많은 도움이 되고 있어

supportive = helpful

046 **She's very unhappy right now**

걘 지금 무척 불행해

047 **Should I bring my girlfriend?**

내 여친 데려와야 돼?

bring sb는 …을 데려오다

048 **Should I call her?**

걔에게 전화해야 돼?

049 **Should I go there alone?**

거기 혼자 가야 돼?

050 **Should I take a taxi?**

택시를 타야 돼?

take[get] a taxi는 택시를 타다, 택시를 타고 집에 가다는 take a taxi home

051 **So I figured it out**

그래서 알게 되었지

figure out = understand or solve the problem

052 **So what?**

그래서 뭐가 어쨌다고?

= That means nothing to me

053 **So you mean now you're not seeing anyone?**

그럼 지금 사귀는 사람이 없다는 말야?

be seeing sb는 …와 만나다, 사귀다

054 **Some guy just called for you**

방금 어떤 사람한테서 전화왔어

055 **Something's come up**

일이 생겼어

= I have to do something else, so I can't keep our appointment.

056 **Sorry, Jane, I didn't recognize your voice**

미안 제인, 네 목소리를 알아듣지 못했어

057 **Sorry, what did you say?**

죄송하지만 뭐라고 하셨죠?

= Say it again

058 **Sounds fine**

좋아

059 **Sounds interesting**

재미있겠는데

060 **Sounds like a plan!**

좋은 생각이야!

= I think that will be fine

061 **Stop picking on me!**

그만 나 좀 놀려!

pick on sb는 …을 놀리다, 괴롭히다

062 **Stop saying that!**

그만 좀 얘기해!

= Don't repeat it anymore

063 **Suit yourself**

마음대로 해

= Do whatever you want

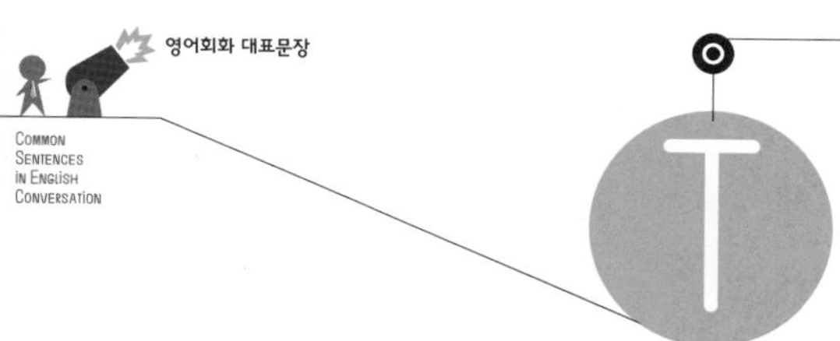

001
Take a day off

하루 쉬어

take a day off는 하루 쉬다

002
Take care of yourself

너 조심해

"행운을 빌어. 몸 조심하고"는 Good luck. Take care of yourself.

003
Take care!

조심하고!

= Goodbye

004
Take it easy

진정해, 잘지내

= Just calm down, Relax, Goodbye

005
Take my word for it

내가 하는 말 좀 잘 들어, 진짜야

= Believe me = Take it from me

006 **Take the subway**

전철을 타

007 **Take this**

이걸로 골라

008 **Take your time**

천천히 해, 서두르지마

= Relax and don't be stressed about a deadline

009 **Tell me about it!**

그러게나 말야!

= I agree with that statement

010 **Thank you for coming**

와줘서 고마워

Thank you for ~ing는 …해줘서 고마워

011 **Thank you for giving me this job**

내게 이 일을 줘서 고마워요

012 **Thank you for saying that**

그렇게 말해줘서 고마워

013 **Thank you for that**

그렇게 해줘서 고마워요

Thank you for~ 다음에 명사가 오는 경우

014 **Thank you for the ride**

태워다줘서 고마워

015 **Thank you for your help**

네가 도와줘서 고마워

016 **Thank you for your time**

시간내줘서 고마워

017 **Thank you in advance**

미리 감사해

in advance는 미리, 사전에

018
Thanks for dinner last night

지난 밤에 저녁 고마워

Thanks = Thank you

019
Thanks for telling me

말해줘서 고마워

020
Thanks for the information

그 정보 알려줘서 고마워

021
Thanks for the advice

조언 고마워

022
Thanks for the tip

귀띔해줘서 고마워

023
That can't be good

안 좋은 징조야

"걔한테 좋을 리가 없어"는 That can't be good for her.

024 **That can't be**

(놀라서) 그럴 리가 없어

= I don't believe it.

025 **That depends**

상황에 따라 달라

= This may change sometime. Depedning on~는 …에 따라서

026 **That explains it**

그러고 보니 이해가 되네

= I see the reason why

027 **That figures**

그럴 줄 알았어

"그럴 줄 알았어. 걘 항상 무척 똑똑했어"는 That figures. She always was very smart.

028 **That hurts**

그거 안됐네

= It seems like a bad thing.

029 **That makes me feel so good**

그 소리를 들으니 기분이 좋군

make sb feel~는 …의 기분을 …하게 만들다

030 **That makes sense**

말되네

make sense는 말이 되다

031 **That reminds me**

그러고 보니 생각나네

= I just remembered something. That reminds me of~는 그 말을 듣고 보니 …가 생각나네

032 **That rings a bell**

얼핏 기억이 나네

= That is familiar to me. "난 못 들어 봤는데"는 It does not ring a bell with me.

033 **That sounds good to me**

난 좋아

sound good to sb는 …에게 좋다

034 **That sounds like a threat**

협박처럼 들리는데

That sounds like+N는 …처럼 들리다

035 **That was a close call**

큰일날 뻔 했어

Something bad almost happened.

036 **That was close**

아슬아슬했어

037 **That was the first time you said that**

네가 그렇게 말한 건 처음이었어

great 대신에, 강조하기 위해 wonderful, perfect 등의 단어를 써도 된다.

038 **That'd be great**

그럼 좋지

039 **That'd be nice[cool]**

(그럼) 멋질거야

That'd = That would

040 **That'll be $450**

450달러입니다

"다 왔습니다, 손님. 5달러 50센트입니다"는 Here we are, sir. That'll be $5.50.

041 **That'll be a big help**

큰 도움이 될거야

"도움이 될거야"는 That'll help.

042 **That'll be fine**

괜찮을거야

043 **That'll do**

그만하면 됐어

= Okay, that worked, now we can leave. "그만하면 됐어. 이제 집에 가봐"는 That will do. You guys can go home now.

044 **That's so sweet**

고마워라, 친절도 해라.

= It was a very kind thing to do.

045 **That's a lie**

그건 거짓야

"아네요. 거짓예요. 그런 적 없어요"는 No way. That's a lie. It never happened.

046 **That's a shame!**

저런!

= That's too bad.

047 **That's a steal!**

거저네!

"바가지야 바가지"는 That's a rip-off.

048 **That's all**

그게 다야

049 **That's all I need to hear**

내가 듣고 싶은 건 그게 다야

"내가 알고 싶은 건 그게 다야"는 That's all I need to know.

050 **That's all right**

괜찮아

all right 대신에 okay를 써도 된다.

051 **That's because all people are selfish**

모든 사람은 다 이기적이어서 그래

That's because S+V는 …하기 때문이야

052 **That's because there is no answer**

답이 없기 때문이야

053 **That's because you don't understand that**

네가 그걸 이해못하기 때문이야

054

That's exactly what I want

그게 바로 내가 원하는거야

That's what S+V~은 S가 V하는 것이 바로 that이라는 의미로 "바로 그게 내가 …하는 거야" 라는 의미

055

That's for sure

확실하지, 물론이지

= You are right about that

056

That's how he died

그렇게 걔가 죽었어

That's how S+V는 그렇게 …하다

057

That's it

바로 그거야, 그만 됐어

"그만 됐어. 오늘 일은 끝냈어"는 That's it. I've finished working for the day.

058

That's more like it

그게 더 낫네요

= I'm happy with how things have changed.

059

That's my favorite

내가 좋아하는거야

060 **That's no excuse**

그건 변명거리가 안 돼

= I don't accept your explanation of why this happened.

061 **That's not how it works**

그렇게는 안돼

= You did it wrong.

062 **That's not how we do things here**

여기서는 그렇게 하는 게 아니야

063 **That's not the point**

핵심은 그게 아니라구

"그게 중요한 게 아니잖아. 중요한 건 내가 불안하다는거야"는 That's not the point. The point is that I don't feel safe.

064 **That's not true**

사실이 아니야

065 **That's not what I meant**

그런 뜻이 아니었어

That's no what I mean은 "실은 그런 뜻은 아냐"

066

That's not what I want

그건 내가 바라는 게 아냐

067

That's not what you think

그건 네 생각과 달라, 속단하지마

= You don't understand it = It's not that(그런게 아냐)

068

That's terrific!

끝내주네!

069

That's the most important thing

그게 가장 중요한거야

070

That's the point

요점은 그거야, 중요한 건 그거야

That's not the point는 "중요한 건 그게 아냐"

071

That's the way it is

다 그런거야

= That's the way it goes = You can't do anything to change it

072 **That's too bad**

정말 안됐어

073 **That's very helpful**

정말 도움이 돼

074 **That's what I mean**

내 말이 그 말야

075 **That's what I thought!**

누가 아니래!, 나도 그렇게 생각했어

= I was sure that was correct.

076 **That's what I was going to say**

바로 그게 내가 말하려고 한거야

077 **That's what I'm saying**

(상대방 말에 동의하며) 내 말이 바로 그거야

= That is the idea I have been talking about.

078 **That's what I'm telling you**

그게 바로 내가 네게 말하는거야

079 **That's what I'm trying to say**

내가 말하려는 건 그게 아냐

080 **That's when I broke my leg**

그때 다리가 부러진거야

That's when S+V는 바로 그때 …하다

081 **That's who Louis talked to**

저 사람이 바로 루이스하고 말 나누던 사람야

That's[This is] who S+V는 저게[저 사람이] 바로 …야, 이게[이 사람이] 바로 …야

082 **That's why I don't want to go tonight**

바로 그래서 오늘밤 가기 싫어

That's why S+V는 바로 그래서 …해

083 **That's why I wanted to talk to you**

바로 그래서 너하고 얘기하고 싶었어

084 **That's why we're here**

그래서 우리가 여기 있는거야

085 **That's why you don't have to worry**

바로 그래서 넌 걱정할 필요가 없어

086 **The most unbelievable thing has happened**

믿기지 않는 일이 벌어졌어

087 **The point is I don't need this right now**

요점은 지금 당장은 그게 필요하지 않는다는거야

"요는 네가 제인과 결혼했다는거지"는 The point is that you're married to Jane.

088 **The police officer had no choice but to use force**

그 경찰관은 무력을 쓸 수밖에 없었어

have no choice but to+V는 …하지 않을 수 없다

089 **The thing is I don't really believe it**

요는 내가 널 안 믿는다는거야

The thing S+V는 중요한 건 …이야

090 **The way I see it**

내가 보기엔

= This is my opinion

091 **There is a lot of work to do here**

여기 할 일이 너무 많아

092 **There is no doubt about it**

확실해 그래

= I'm sure of it

093 **There is no one by the name of John here**

여기엔 존이란 이름의 사람이 없어요

094 **There is not enough time**

시간이 부족해

095 **There is nothing like that**

저 만한 게 없지

= That thing is very special. No, nothing like that은 "아냐, 그런 건 아냐"

096 **There is some problem with the cell phone**

핸드폰에 좀 문제가 있어

097 **There must be a bad connection**

연결상태가 안좋은가봐

= We have a bad connection. "소리가 끊어져서 들려요"는 You're breaking up

098 **There never seems to be enough money**

돈이란 늘 부족한 것 같아

099 **There seem to be an accident**

사고가 있었던 것 같아

100 **There used to be a big tree in the park**

예전엔 공원에 큰 나무가 있었는데

There used to+V는 과거에 …가 있었다

101 **There you go again**

또 시작이로구만

= I'm tired of hearing you say that so many times.

102 **There's a chance he can get better**

걔가 나아질 가능성이 있어

There's a chance S+V는 …할 가능성이 있다

103 **There's a chance**

가능성이 있어

104 **There's a good chance you will fail**

실패할 가능성이 커

There's a good chance S+V는 …할 가능성이 크다

105 **There's a phone call for you**

전화왔어

간단히 Phone call for you라고 해도 된다.

106 **There's no excuse for it**

그건 변명의 여지가 없어

107 **There's no hard feelings on my part**

악의는 아냐

간단히 No hard feelings라고 해도 된다. = I'm not angry.

108 **There's no hurry**

급할 거 없어

= There's no rush.

109 **There's no need to go now**

이제 갈 필요 없어

There's no need to+V는 …할 필요가 없다

110 **There's no telling what you think**

네가 뭘 생각하는 지 알 수가 없어

There's no telling what[how] S+V는 …을 알 수가 없어

111 **There's no way I can do that**

그렇게 하는 건 불가능해

(There's) No way S+V는 …을 할 수가 없어

112 **There's no way she's going to make it**

걔가 성공할 리가 없어

make it은 해내다, 성공하다

113 **There's no way to decide who's going to stay**

누가 남을지 결정할 방법이 없어

There's no way to+V 역시 …을 할 수가 없어

114 **There's no way to repair the car**

이 차를 수리할 수가 없어

repair the car는 차를 수리하다

115 **There's no way you can finish the job on time**

네가 그 일을 제시간에 끝낼 수가 없어

finish sth on time은 제시간에 …을 끝내다

116 **There's no way you're going to talk me into this**

네가 날 설득해서 그걸 하게 할 수 없어

take sb into sth은 …을 설득하여 …하게 하다

117 **There's something you should know**

네가 알아야 될게 있어

There's something S+V는 …하는게 좀 있어

118 **There's nothing to worry about**

걱정할 것 하나도 없어

= There is no reason to be upset.

119 **They are so different**

그것들은 너무 달라

120 **They are so stupid**

걔네들은 정말 멍청해

121 **They get excited when they see famous people**

유명인들을 보면 사람들은 흥분해

get excited = be excited

122 **They took Ben to the park**

걔들이 벤을 공원에 데리고 갔어

take sb to+장소는 …을 …로 데리고 가다

123 **Things are getting better**

사정이 점점 좋아지고 있어

be getting better는 점점 나아지고 있다

124 **Think nothing of it**

그렇게 생각하지마, 맘쓰지마

감사하다고 혹은 미안하다고 하는 상대방에게

125 **This doesn't taste as good as it looks**

보기처럼 맛있지 않아

126 **This is for you**

이거 네거야

뭔가 건네주면서

127 **This is going to be so much fun**

이건 무척 재미있을거야

128 **This is going to be tough**

이건 힘들거야

tough 대신 hard를 써도 된다.

129 **This is just what I wanted**

내가 원했던 게 바로 이거야

This is what S+V는 이게 바로 …하는거야

130 **This is much better**

훨씬 나아

131 **This is my first time to come here**

난 여기 오는 건 처음이야

This is my first time to+V는 …하는 것은 처음이야

132 **This is my treat**

이건 내가 낼게

간단히 My treat라고 해도 된다. I'll treat you 역시 "내가 쏠게"

133 **This is not my day**

일진이 안좋네

= I think I'm going to have problems today. 반대는 This is my day.

134 **This is really important to me**

이건 정말 내게 중요해

135 **This is so much fun**

이건 무척 재미있다

136 **This is something I'd rather do alone**

이건 내가 혼자 하는게 나은거야

I'd rather+V는 차라리 …하는게 나아

137 **This is the first time I go to a night club**

내가 나이트 클럽에 가는 건 처음이야

night club은 콩글리쉬가 아니다.

138 **This is the most special day of our lives**

우리 인생에서 가장 의미있는 날이야

139 **This is too much**

이건 너무해

This is too much for+N (to do)는 …에게는 (하기가) 너무 힘들다

140 **This is unbelievable**

정말 말도 안돼

unbelievable 대신에 ridiculous를 써도 된다.

141 **This is what I want to do**

이게 바로 내가 하고 싶은거야

This is what~은 "이게 바로 내가 …하는 거야"라는 의미

142 **This is what I was afraid of**

이게 바로 내가 걱정했던거야

be afraid of는 걱정하다, 무서워하다

143 **This is what I'm talking about**

이게 바로 내가 말하는거야

talk about sth은 …에 관해 얘기나누다

144 **This is what you have to do**

이게 바로 네가 해야 하는거야

have to = must

145 **This is what you're looking for**

이게 바로 네가 찾던거야

look for는 …을 찾다

146 **This is where I live**

내가 사는 곳이 바로 여기야

This is where S+V는 바로 여기가 …하는 곳이야

147 **This is where we first met**

여기가 우리가 처음 만난 곳이야

148 **This is where you put it?**

여기에 네가 그것을 놓은거야?

149 **This is where you work?**

여기가 네가 일하는 곳이야?

150

This is who we are. This is our lives

이게 바로 우리야. 이게 우리 인생이지

This is who S+V는 이게[이 사람이] 바로 …야

151

This isn't fair

이건 공평치 않아

152

This looks like a really nice place

아주 멋있는 곳 같아

look like+N는 …처럼 보이다

153

Time flies!

세월 참 빠르구나!

= How times flies!

154

Turn right at the intersection

교차로에서 우회전해요

"다음 코너에서 우회전해요"는 Turn right at the next corner.

CHECK IT OUT! 문장속에서 확인해보기!

A: When do you want it delivered?
B: There's no hurry.
A: How about at the end of the week?

A: 그걸 언제쯤 배달해 드리면 될까요?
B: 급할 거 없습니다.
A: 주말이면 어떻겠습니까?

★ want it delivered
want ~ pp의 패턴으로 「…을 …하기를 원하다」라는 의미

A: We got mail today and **this is for you**.
B: Please put it on my desk, I'm busy right now.
A: Alright, but don't forget to open it.

A: 오늘 우편물이 왔는데, 이건 당신 앞으로 온 거에요.
B: 제 책상에 두세요, 지금 바빠서요.
A: 그러죠, 잊지 말고 꼭 열어보세요.

★ put it on~
가장 기본적인 의미로 쓰인 put으로 「…을 …위에 놓다」라는 의미이다.

A: I can't wait to see the new play.
B: Same here. I bought tickets last night.
A: Let's go together and grab dinner before.

A: 새로 시작하는 연극을 빨리 보고 싶어.
B: 나도 그래. 어젯 밤에 표를 샀어.
A: 같이 가서 그 전에 저녁부터 먹자.

★ go together and+V
go togehter and+V의 패턴으로 「함께 모여서 …하다」라는 의미로, 모여서 무엇을 하는지는 and+V의 형태로 이어주면 된다.

A: Guess what? It's raining out.
B: So what?
A: So we can't go to the beach, that's what.

A: 저기 말야. 밖에 비가 와.
B: 그래서 뭐 어쨌다고?
A: 그렇게 되면 우린 바닷가에 갈 수 없게 된다구.

★Guess what?
뭔가 새로운 소식을 전할 때 꺼내말 어구.

A: Do you have time to have dinner?
B: Not really, I think I must be going now.
A: That's too bad. I was hoping you'd stay for dinner.

A: 저녁 먹을 시간 있어요?
B: 실은 안 돼요. 지금 가봐야 될 것 같아요.
A: 그렇군요. 남아서 식사하시기를 바랬는데요.

★have dinner
식사명 앞에서는 관사를 붙이지 않는다는 점을 주의한다.

A: I can't come to your house tonight.
B: Do you mean you won't be coming over for dinner?
A: That's right. I've got soccer practice.

A: 오늘밤에 너희 집에 못가.
B: 저녁 먹으러 못 온다는 말야?
A: 그래. 축구 연습이 있어서.

★won't
will not의 축약형으로 발음은 [wount]라 한다.

U
V
W
X
U-W

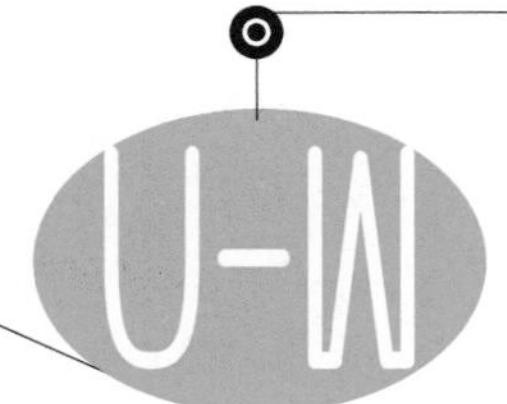

001 **Use your head!**

머리를 쓰라고!

= Consider it carefully.

002 **Want some more?**

더 먹을래?

앞에 Do you~가 생략된 것. "좀 더 들어"는 Have some more.

003 **Watch your tongue!**

(어린이에게) 말 조심해!

= Be careful of what you say because you are saying bad things.

004 **Way to go!**

잘한다!, 잘해!

"잘했어, 아들아! 난 네가 그걸 발견할 줄 알았어"는 Way to go son! I knew you'd find it!

005 **We appreciate your hospitality**

환대해줘서 고마워

appreciate sth은 …을 감사하다

006 **We are always being asked to work late**

늘상 우리에게 야근을 시켜

be asked to+V는 …하라고 요청받다

007 **We can't afford to live here anymore**

우리는 더 이상 여기서 살 여력이 없어

can't afford to+V는 …할 여력이 없다

008 **We decided to have a baby**

우린 애를 갖기로 했어

"걔가 애를 낳았어"는 She had a baby.

009 **We didn't come here to hurt you**

네게 상처를 주려고 온 게 아니야

come here to+V는 …하려고 여기 오다

010 **We don't have enough money to do that**

그렇게 할 돈이 충분하지 않아

have enough money to+V는 …할 돈이 충분하다

011 **We haven't thought about that stuff**

그거에 대해 생각해본 적이 없어

012

We hope you all have a very merry Christmas

너희 모두 즐거운 성탄절 되길 바래

013

We need to clean this place up

여기를 깨끗이 청소해야 돼

clean~ up은 깨끗이 청소하다

014

We run out of gas

기름이 없어

run out of = run short of = be short of는 …가 부족하다, 떨어지다

015

We should make do with it

이걸로라도 때워야 돼

= We need to do the best we can. make do with는 그런대로 …로 때우다, 변통하다

016

We should try to be more social with people

사람들과 더 잘 어울리도록 해야

be social with sb는 …와 잘 어울리다

017

We used to play together all the time

우린 항상 함께 놀았었지

all the time = always

018 **We went to a Mets game**

우린 메츠 게임 갔었어

019 **We'd better call the fire department**

소방서에 전화해야 돼

call+기관은 …에 전화하다. call to+기관이 아니다. call 다음에 to가 올 경우는 call to+V

020 **We'd better go. The movie starts in 30 minutes**

우린 가야 돼. 영화가 30분 후에 시작해

had better+V는 …하는게 나아

021 **We'll be all right if we work together**

우리가 함께 일한다면 문제 없을거야

work together는 함께 일하다

022 **We'll get it to you as fast as we possibly can**

가능한 빨리 가져다 드리죠

023 **We'll give a call if anything comes up**

무슨 일 있으면 전화줄게요

~come up은 갑작스럽게 예상치 못한 일이 생기다

024

We're done for the day

퇴근하자

be done for the day = be gone for the day

025

We're going to have fun tonight!

우리 오늘밤에 재미있게 놀거다!

have fun은 재미있게 놀다

026

We're well aware of your problem

네 문제를 우린 잘 알고 있어

be aware of~는 …을 잘 알고 있다

027

We've been planning this for months

우린 이걸 오랫동안 계획해왔어

028

We've got a problem

우린 문제가 있어

029

We've never done this before

우린 전에 이걸 해본 적이 없어

"이거 해본 적 한번도 없어. 어떻게 해야 할지 모르겠어"는 I've never done this before. I don't know what I'm doing.

030 **Well, we finished cleaning the house**

저기, 집청소 다했어

finish ~ing는 …을 끝내다

031 **We're already 30 minutes behind schedule**

이미 예정보다 30분 늦었어

behind scedule은 예정보다 늦게, ahead of schedule은 예정보다 빨리, 그리고 on schedule은 예정에 맞게

032 **What a coincidence!**

이런 우연이!

= It's surprising that these things happened.

033 **What a disappointment!**

참 실망스럽네!

034 **What a great idea!**

야 참 좋은 생각이야!

035 **What a shame!**

안됐구나!

What a relief!는 참 다행이야!, What a pity!는 저런!

A-D E-H I-K L-P S-T U-W Y

036

What a small world!

세상 참 좁네!

= I'm surprised that these things are related.

037

What a surprise!

정말 놀랍군!

038

What am I supposed to do?

내가 어떻게 해야 되지?

be supposed to+V는 …하기로 되어 있다

039

What are friends for?

친구 좋다는 게 뭐야?

"그래서 친구가 있는거지"는 That's what friends are for.

040

What are you doing after work?

퇴근 후에 뭐해?

"이번 주말에 뭐 할거야?"는 What are you doing this weekend?

041

What are you doing here?

여긴 어쩐 일이야?

= Why did you come?

042 **What are you going to do if we win?**

우리가 이기면 어떻게 할거야?

What are you going to do if[when] S+V?는 …하면 어떻게 할거야?

043 **What are you going to do when you see her?**

걜 보면 어떻게 할거야?

044 **What are you going to do with the letter?**

그 편지 어떻게 할거야?

What are you going to do with sth?은 …을 어떻게 할거야?

045 **What are you going to do?**

어떻게 할거야?

"그거 어떻게 할거야?"는 What are you going do about that?

046 **What are you going to have?**

뭘 드시겠어요?

What would you like to have?라고 해도 된다.

047 **What are you going to say?**

뭐라고 말할거야?

"걔에게 뭐라고 할거야?"는 What are you going to tell her?

048 **What are you looking for?**

뭐 찾는거야?

049 **What are you saying?**

(놀람, 반대) 무슨 말이야?

= I don't think that is right.

050 **What are you talking about?**

(놀람, 황당) 무슨 말이야?

= I don't understnad what you mean.

051 **What are you trying to say?**

무슨 말을 하려는거야?

= Tell it to me directly.

052 **What are you up to?**

뭐해?

"그래 뭐해? 쇼핑 좀 하는 거야?"는 So what are you up to? Doing a little shopping?

053 **What brings you here?**

무슨 일로 온거야?

"무슨 일로 병원에 왔어?" What brings you to the hospital?

054 **What can I do for you?**

뭘 도와줄까요?

= Can I help you?

055 **What can I do to help her?**

걜 도와주기 위해 어떻게 해야 할까?

"내가 더 도와줄 일 없어?"는 What else can I do for you?

056 **What can I do to make it up to you?**

어떻게 하면 이 실수를 만회할 수 있을까요?

make it up to sb는 …에게 보상하다, 만회하다

057 **What can I do?**

내가 (달리) 어쩌겠어?

= I don't think I can do anything. "난들 어쩌겠어? 걔의 선택인데"는 What can I do? It is his choice.

058 **What can I get you?**

뭘 갖다 줄까?

059 **What can I help you with?**

무엇을 도와 드릴까요?

help sb with sth는 …가 …하는 것을 도와주다

060

What can I order for you?

뭘 주문하시겠습니까?

061

What can I say?

난 할 말이 없네, 나더러 어쩌라는거야, 뭐랄까?

= I'm not sure what to say. "글쎄 뭐라고 할까? 네가 맞았고 내가 틀렸어"는 What can I say? You were right, I was wrong.

062

What can I tell you?

어찌라고?, 뭐라고 해야 하나?

= I don't have an excuse. "뭐라 해야 하나? 뜻하지 않게 망가트렸어"는 What can I tell you? I accidentally broke it.

063

What comes with that?

뭐가 따라나오나요?

"점심 특식에는 뭐가 함께 나오나요?"는 What comes with the lunch special?

064

What did you buy?

뭐 샀어?

065

What did you do to my dad?

내 아버지한테 어떻게 한거야?

What did you do to sb?는 …에게 어떻게 한거야?

066 **What did you do with it?**

그거 어떻게 했어?

"아스피린 어떻게 했어?"는 What did you do with the aspirin?

067 **What did you do?**

어떻게 한거야? , 뭘 한거야?

"닉, 지난 밤에 뭐했어?"는 What did you do last night, Nick?

068 **What did you get for her?**

걔에게 뭘 사줬어?

get은 갖다주다, 사주다

069 **What did you get for your birthday?**

생일 선물로 뭘 받았어?

070 **What did you say?**

뭐라고요?

"걔한테 뭐라고 했니?"는 What did you say to him?

071 **What did you think I was going to do?**

내가 뭘 할거라 생각했어?

072 **What do you call that in English?**

저걸 영어로는 뭐라고 하니?

call sth in English는 영어로 …라 부르다

073 **What do you do?**

직업이 뭐야?

뒤에 for a living을 넣어도 된다.

074 **What do you know about her?**

그 여자에 대해 아는 게 뭐야?

What do you know about +N/S+V?는 …에 대해 네가 뭘 알아?

075 **What do you know?**

놀랍군, 네가 뭘 안다고!

= I don't think you know much about that.

076 **What do you mean, no?**

아니라는 게 무슨 말이야?

"너무 늦었다니 그게 무슨 말이야?"는 What do you mean too late?

077 **What do you mean by that?**

그게 무슨 말이야?

상대방이 말한 내용을 다시 언급하지 않고 그냥 간단히 by that으로 쓴 경우

078 **What do you mean you don't remember me?**

나를 기억못한다니 그게 무슨 말이야?

What do you mean S+V?는 …하다니 그게 무슨 말야?

079 **What do you mean you got fired? What happened?**

잘렸다니 그게 무슨 말이야? 무슨 일이야?

get fired는 해고 당하다

080 **What do you mean you quit?**

그만 둔다니 그게 무슨 말이야?

quit은 그만두다 = quit one's job

081 **What do you mean you're going to London?**

런던으로 간다니 그게 무슨 말이야?

082 **What do you mean you're not coming?**

네가 못온다니 그게 무슨 말이야?

083 **What do you mean you're not so sure?**

확실하지 않다니 무슨 말이야?

084 **What do you mean?**

그게 무슨 말이야?

085 **What do you need?**

뭐가 필요해?

상대방이 뭐 필요한지 물어보는 말

086 **What do you say I buy you a cup of coffee?**

내가 커피한잔 사면 어때?

What do you say (that) S+V?는 …가 어때?

087 **What do you say I take you to dinner tonight?**

오늘 밤 저녁먹으러 갈래?

088 **What do you say to going for a drink?**

오늘밤 한잔 하러 가는거 어때요?

What do you say to +N[~ing]?는 …하는 거 어때?

089 **What do you say we call it a night and get some sleep?**

이제 그만 끝내고 잠을 좀 자는 게 어때?

call it a night[day]는 그만두다, get some sleep은 잠 좀 자다

090 **What do you say we get together for a drink?**

만나서 술한잔 하면 어때?

get together for a drink는 만나서 술한잔하다

091 **What do you say we go take a walk?**

가서 산책하면 어때?

talk a walk는 산보하다

092 **What do you say we take a break?**

좀 쉬는 게 어때?

take a break은 잠시 쉬다

093 **What do you say?**

어때?

"6시 30분 내집에서 어때?"는 What do you say, 6:30, my place?

094 **What do you take me for?**

날 뭘로 보는거야?

= Do you think I'm foolish?

095 **What do you think about me staying the night?**

내가 밤새 머무르는거 어때?

What do you think about sb ~ing?는 …가 …하는 것을 어떻게 생각해?

096 **What do you think about my idea?**

내 생각이 어때?

What do you think about sth?은 …는 어때?

097 **What do you think he looks like?**

걔 외모가 어떤 것 같아?

098 **What do you think I am?**

날 뭘로 보는 거야? (내가 뭐하는 사람 같아?)

099 **What do you think of adding him to our team?**

걔를 우리 팀에 넣으면 어때?

What do you think of+N[~ing]?는 …하면 어때?

100 **What do you think of that?**

저거 어떻게 생각해?

= How do you feel about it?

101 **What do you think of Wendy?**

웬디를 어떻게 생각해?

102 **What do you think she wants?**

걔가 뭘 원하는 것 같아

What do you think (S+) V?는 …하다고 생각해?

103 **What do you think will happen?**

어떻게 될 것 같아?

104 **What do you think you're doing?**

너 정신 나갔냐?(이게 무슨 짓이야?)

= Why are you doing that?

105 **What do you think?**

네 생각은 어때?

106 **What do you want for your birthday?**

생일 때 뭐 갖고 싶어?

107 **What do you want from me?**

나보고 어쩌라고?

108
What do you want me to do?

날 더러 어쩌라고?

Want 다음에 to do의 의미상 주어인 me가 나온 경우로 상대방에게 뭘 원하냐고 물어보는 것이 아니라 내가 뭘하기를 네가 원하냐고 물어보는 표현이다.

109
What do you want me to say?

날 더러 뭘 말하라고?

"나보고 어쩌라고? 내가 나쁜 엄마라고 말하라는거야?"는 What do you want me to say? You want me to say I'm a bad mother?

110
What do you want to do first?

제일 먼저 뭐하고 싶어?

111
What do you want to do with it?

그거 어떻게 하고 싶어?

What do you want to do with sth?은 …을 어떻게 하고 싶어?

112
What do you want to do?

뭘 하고 싶은데?, 어떻게 할거야?

want 다음에는 to+동사, 혹은 for+명사가 와서 …을 원하느냐, 혹은 …을 하고 싶어라는 의미가 된다

113
What do you want to know about Angela?

안젤라에 대해 뭘 알고 싶어?

What do you want to know about~?은 …에 대해 뭘 알고 싶어?

114 **What do you want to know?**

뭘 알고 싶어?

115 **What do you want to say?**

무슨 말 하고 싶어?

116 **What do you want to talk about?**

무슨 얘기하고 싶은거야?

117 **What do you want?**

뭘 원해?

"내가 원하는 건 신경쓰지마. 네가 원하는 건 뭐야?"는 Never mind what I want. What do you want?

118 **What does he look like? Is he cute?**

걔 어때? 귀여워?

119 **What else could I do?**

그 수밖에 더 있겠어?

120

What for?

왜, 뭐 때문에?

= Tell me the reason

121

What happened at work?

직장에서 무슨 일 있었어?

"저녁 때 어떻게 된거야?"는 What happened at dinner?

122

What happened last night?

간밤에 무슨 일이야?

123

What happened to her?

걔한테 무슨 일이 있는 거야?

What happened to[with] sb?는 …에게 무슨 일이야?

124

What happened to the dinner party?

저녁파티는 어떻게 된거야?

What happened to sth?은 …은 어떻게 된거야?

125

What happened to the documents I left here?

내가 여기 둔 문서는 어떻게 됐어?

126 **What happened to your date?**

데이트 어떻게 된거야?

127 **What happened?**

무슨 일이야?, 어떻게 된거야?

128 **What have you been up to?**

어떻게 지냈어?, 무슨 일 있었어?

= Have you been doing anything interesting lately?

129 **What I'm saying is I'm not an expert**

내 말은 난 전문가는 아니란 말이야

What I'm saying is S+V는 내 말은 …라는거야

130 **What I'm saying is Kate likes you**

내 말은 케이트가 널 좋아한다는거야

131 **What I'm trying to say is that he's rich**

내가 하려는 말은 걔가 부자라는거야

What I'm trying to say is S+V는 내가 하려는 말은 …라는거야

132 **What is he taking TOEIC for?**

걘 왜 토익을 보려는거야

What ~ for? = Why~?

133 **What is that like?**

그거 어떤거야?

What ~ like?는 How~?. 즉 '명사'가 어떠냐고 물어보는 것으로 사람[사물]의 성격[성질]이 어떤지 물어보는 것이고 What does A look like?는 단순히 외관이 어떤지를 물어보는 것이다.

134 **What is your new house like?**

새로 이사한 집 어때?

135 **What kind of car are you going to buy?**

어떤 종류의 차를 살거야?

What이 단독이 아니라 뒤에 명사를 붙여서 의문문을 만드는 경우

136 **What kind of information?**

어떤 종류의 정보야?

137 **What kind of music does your wife like?**

네 아내는 어떤 종류의 음악을 좋아해?

138 **What kind of party was that?**

어떤 종류의 파티였어?

139 **What kind of plans?**

어떤 종류의 계획야?

140 **What made you change your mind?**

뭐 때문에 마음을 바꾼거야?

What made you+V? = Why did you+V?

141 **What makes you say that?**

왜 그렇게 말하는 거야?

What makes you + V ~?는 직역하면 무엇(What)이 너(you)로 하여금 …하게 만들었나?로 결국 형식은 What으로 시작했지만 내용은 이유를 묻는 말로 Why do you+V?와 같은 의미

142 **What makes you so sure?**

어떻게 그렇게 확신해?

= You need to explain why you believe that.

143 **What makes you so sure I don't have talent?**

왜 내가 재능이 없다고 확신하는거야?

What makes you so sure S+V?는 왜 …라고 확신하는거야?

A-D E-H I-K L-P S-T U-W Y

144

What makes you think so?

왜 그렇게 생각하니?

"왜 걔가 프로포즈할 거라 생각한거야?"는 What makes you think he's going to propose?

145

What makes you think there's a difference?

차이가 있다고 왜 생각하는거야?

What makes you think S+V?는 왜 …라고 생각하는거야?

146

What number did you dial?

몇 번에 거셨습니까?

147

What seems to be the problem?

어디가 아파?

148

What should I do?

내가 어떻게 해야 하지?

= Can you tell me your opinion?

149

What time are we supposed to leave?

우리는 몇 시에 떠나야 돼?

What+명사의 또다른 경우로 time이 온 패턴이다.

150 **What time did you get there?**

넌 몇 시에 거기에 도착했어?

get there은 도착하다

151 **What time do you want to pick me up?**

몇 시에 날 픽업할거야?

pick sb up은 차로 픽업하다

152 **What time does Tom start work?**

탐이 몇 시에 일하기 시작했어?

153 **What time does your mom get back from work?**

네 엄마는 언제 퇴근하셔?

154 **What time would be good for you?**

몇시가 좋겠어?

155 **What took you so long?**

왜 이렇게 오래 걸렸어?

= Why were you late?

156
What was her name?

걔 이름이 뭐였지?

157
What was that sound?

저게 무슨 소리지?

158
What was that? Have you ever seen anything like that?

저게 뭐였어? 저런 거 본 적 있어?

159
What would you do if you were in her situation?

네가 걔처지라면 어떻게 하겠어?

What would you do if ~는 …라면 넌 어떻게 하겠냐?

160
What're you going to do?

어쩔거야?

"어쩔건대? 고소라도 할거야?"는 What're you going to do? Sue me?, "어쩔건대? 거짓말했다고 체포할거야?"는 What're you going to do? Arrest me for telling a lie?

161
What's bothering you?

뭐가 잘못됐어?

What's bugging you? = What's bothering you? = What's troubling you? 뭐가 문제야?

162 **What's cooking?**

무슨 일이야?

오래된 슬랭으로 = What's going on?

163 **What's eating you?**

뭐가 문제야?, 무슨 걱정거리라도 있어?

= What's bothering you?

164 **What's going on?**

무슨 일이야?

"침착해. 무슨 일이야?"는 Just calm down. What's going on?

165 **What's got into you?**

뭣때문에 이러는거야?

= Why are you being odd?

166 **What's happening?**

무슨 일이야?

"무슨 일이야? 도대체 무슨 일이야?"는 What's happening? What's this all about?

167 **What's it for?**

무슨 이유로?, 무엇 때문에?

168 **What's new with you?**

넌 어때?

인사표현인 What's new?에 대한 대답

169 **What's on the fifth floor?**

5층에 뭐가 있어?

"오늘 밤에 TV에서 뭐해?"는 What's on TV tonight?

170 **What's on the menu?**

메뉴에 뭐가 있어?

171 **What's on your mind?**

무슨 얘기인데?, 무슨 일인데?

172 **What's the big deal?**

별거 아니네?, 무슨 큰일이라도 있는 거야?

big을 빼고 What's the deal?하면 현재 무슨 일이 벌어지는지 그 이유를 물어보는 표현

173 **What's the bottom line?**

요점이 뭐야?

"요점은 …이야"는 The bottom line is (that) S+V

174 **What's the catch?**

무슨 속셈이야?

= What is the hidden problem with this?

175 **What's the damage?**

얼마예요?

176 **What's the difference?**

그게 무슨 상관이야?

177 **What's the harm?**

손해볼 게 뭐야?, 밑질거 없어

= I don't think this will hurt anything. "…해서 손해보는 게 뭔데?"는 What's the harm in+N[~ing]?

178 **What's the hurry?**

왜 그렇게 서둘러?

= What's the rush?

179 **What's the matter with you?**

무슨 일이야?, 도대체 왜 그래?

= What is your problem?

180 **What's the[your] point?**

요점이 뭐야?

"…하는 의미가 뭐야?, 뭐하러 …하는거야?"는 What's the point of ~ing/N?

181 **What's the price?**

얼마예요?

182 **What's the problem?**

무슨 일이야?

What's the problem with sb[sth]?는 …가 무슨 문제야?

183 **What's the reason for quitting?**

그만두는 이유가 뭐야?

What's the reason for~?는 …이유가 뭐야?

184 **What's the special of the day?**

오늘의 스페셜은 뭔가요?

185 **What's the weather like in Korea?**

한국 날씨는 어때요?

"새로운 매니저 어때?"는 What's the new manager like?

186 **What's the rush?**

왜 이리 급해?

the 대신에 your를 넣어도 된다.

187 **What's with the face?**

얼굴이 왜 그래?

What is with sth?은 …가 왜 그래?

188 **What's with you?**

뭣땜에 그래?

= Why are you acting strangely?

189 **What's wrong with being nice to him?**

걔한테 잘해주는 게 뭐 잘못됐어?

What's wrong with ~ing?는 …하는게 뭐 잘못됐어?

190 **What's wrong with what I'm wearing?**

내가 입고 있는 옷이 뭐 잘못됐어?

What's wrong with~ ?는 …하는게 뭐 잘못됐어?

191 **What's wrong? Are you okay?**

무슨 일이야? 괜찮아?

What' wrong 뒤에 with you를 붙여도 된다.

192

What's wrong with your car?

네 차 뭐가 문제야?

"그게 뭐가 잘 못 된거야?" What's wrong with it?

193

What's your budget?

예산은 얼마로 잡고 계시는데요?

194

What's your suggestion?

네 제안은 뭐야?

195

Whatever you ask

뭐든지 말만 해

Whatever you say는 뭐든 말만해 = I'll agree to any of your suggestions

196

When are you coming back?

언제 돌아오는거야?

come back은 돌아오다

197

When are you getting married?

언제 결혼할거야?

get married는 결혼하다라는 동작중심의 표현

198 **When are you going to do it?**

언제 그럴건데?

199 **When are you going to get a job?**

취직은 언제 할거야?

get a job는 일자리를 얻다, 즉 취직하다

200 **When are you going to tell me?**

언제 내게 말할거야?

201 **When are you leaving for Europe?**

유럽으로 언제 가는거야?

leave for+장소명사는 …을 향해 여기를 출발하다

202 **When are you planning to do this?**

언제 이걸 하려고 해?

be planning to+V는 …할 생각이다

203 **When did you get that?**

그거 언제 구한거야?

A-D E-H I-K L-P S-T U-W Y

204 **When did you meet her?**

쟤를 언제 만났어?

205 **When did you see him last?**

걔를 마지막으로 본게 언제야?

206 **When did you stop smoking?**

담배 언제 끊었어?

stop ~ing는 …을 그만두다, stop to+V는 …하기 위해 멈춰서다

207 **When do you think she's going to get here?**

걔가 언제 여기 올 것 같아?

When do you think S + V?는 네 생각엔 언제 …할(한) 거지?

208 **When do you think we lost her?**

언제 그 여자를 잃어버린 것 같아?

209 **When do you want to go?**

언제 가고 싶어?

When do you want to+V~?는 언제 …하고 싶어?

210 **When do you want to meet him?**

걔를 언제 만나고 싶어?

211 **When does she get here?**

걔가 언제 여기 와?

get here = come

212 **When does the movie start?**

영화가 언제 시작해?

213 **When does the store open?**

가게가 언제 열어?

214 **When is that?**

그게 언제야?

When is+N?는 …가 언제야?

215 **When was the trip?**

여행은 언제였어?

When was+N?는 …가 언제였어?

216 **When we get any new information, I'll let you know**

뭐 새로운 정보를 알게 되면 알려줄게

217 **When were you planning to tell us?**

언제 우리에게 말하려고 했어?

218 **When's a good time?**

언제 좋은 시간이야?

219 **When's she getting home?**

걘 언제 집에 와?

get home은 집에 오다

220 **When's the check-in time?**

체크인이 언제예요?

221 **When's the last time you saw her?**

마지막으로 걜 본 게 언제야?

"걔가 마지막으로 여기 온 게 언제였어?"는 When was the last time she was here?

222 **When's the next flight to New York?**

뉴욕 행 다음 비행편이 언제예요?

223 **When's the party?**

파티가 언제야?

224 **When's the wedding?**

결혼식이 언제야?

"생일이 언제야?"는 When's your birthday?

225 **Where are the keys?**

열쇠 어디에 있어?

226 **Where are these people from?**

이 사람들 어디 출신이예요?

Where is/are+S+ from?는 …는 어디 출신이야, …가 어디서 난거야?

227 **Where are you calling from?**

어디서 전화하는거야?

"어디에서 출발할 예정입니까?"는 Where are you departing from?

A-D E-H I-K L-P S-T U-W Y

228 **Where are you driving to now?**

지금 어디로 차를 몰고 가는거야?

229 **Where are you getting this?**

이거 어디서 났어?

230 **Where are you going to do it?**

어디서 그걸 할 거야?

Where are you going to+V?는 어디에서 …할 겁니까?

231 **Where are you going?**

어디가?

Where과 진행형 시제인 be ~ing가 합쳐진 경우인데 사용빈도는 동사 go를 이용한 Where are you going?이 압도적이다.

232 **Where are you taking me?**

나를 어디로 데려가는 거야?

"점심먹으러 어디로 데려갈거야?"는 Where are you taking me for lunch?

233 **Where are you taking my car?**

내 차 어디로 가져가는 거야?

234 **Where are you traveling to?**

어디로 여행가는거야?

235 **Where can I buy you dinner?**

어디가서 저녁 사줄까?

Where에 조동사인 can, should 등이 결합되는 경우인데 대부분 주어는 일인칭으로 쓰여 Where can I(we) ~?, Where should I(we)~ ?의 형태로 쓰인다.

236 **Where can I drop you?**

어디에 내려줄까?

"어디 가야 걔를 볼 수 있죠?"는 Where can I find her?

237 **Where can I get a taxi?**

어디서 택시 탈 수 있어요?

get a taxi = take a taxi는 택시를 타다

238 **Where can I get tickets to see the show?**

이 공연의 관람티켓을 어디서 구해요?

239 **Where can I go to check my e-mail?**

어디 가서 이메일을 볼 수 있나요?

check one's email은 이멜을 확인하다

240 **Where can I meet you?**

어디서 만날까?

241 **Where can I reach you if there is an emergency?**

급한 일이 생기면 어디로 연락해야 하죠?

…에게 연락하다는 reach sb

242 **Where did you get it?**

그거 어디서 난거야?

"어디서 찾았어?"는 Where did you find it?

243 **Where did you hear that?**

그거 어디서 들었어?

244 **Where did you pick up that computer?**

저 컴퓨터 어디서 구했어?

pick up = buy

245 **Where did you come from?**

어디 출신이야?

246 **Where do you get your hair cut?**

어디서 머리를 깍은거야?

get one's hair cut은 get sth+pp의 구문

247 **Where do you keep it?**

그건 어디에 보관해?

248 **Where do you think I'm going?**

내가 어디에 가는 것 같아?

Where do you think S+V?는 어디에(로) …한다고 생각해?

249 **Where do you think it came from?**

그게 어디에서 났다고 생각해?

come from는 출신 뿐만아니라 출처를 말하기도 한다.

250 **Where do you think she went?**

걔가 어디에 갔다고 생각해?

251 **Where do you want to go to lunch?**

점심 먹으러 어디 가고 싶어?

Where do you want to+V?는 어디서 …하고 싶어?

252

Where do you want to go?

어디 가고 싶어?

253

Where have you been?

어디 갔다 오는 거야?, 어디 갔었어?

"어디갔었어? 전화했는데! 얘기 좀 하자!"는 Where have you been?! I tried to call you! I want to talk to you!

254

Where is this beautiful rug from?

이렇게 아름다운 양탄자를 어디서 구했어?

"이렇게 엄청나게 맛난 케익을 어디서 샀어요?"는 Where is this incredible cake from?

255

Where is the fitting room?

탈의실이 어디죠?

"가장 가까운 레스토랑이 어디야?"는 Where is the nearest restaurant?, "가장 가까운 약국이 어디야?"는 Where's the nearest drug store?

256

Where should we go?

어디로 가지?

257

Where should we start first?

어디부터 시작해야 하지?

258 **Where should we begin?**

어디부터 시작해야 하죠?

259 **Where was I?**

내가 어디까지 얘기했지?

= I forgot the place I stopped talking = Where were we?

260 **Where's everybody?**

다들 어디 있어?

261 **Where's the rest room?**

화장실이 어디야?

"노트북 어디 있니?" Where's your lap top computer?

262 **Where's your passport?**

네 여권이 어디에 있어?

263 **Which coat do you like best?**

어떤 코트를 가장 좋아해?

Which+N do you like best?는 어떤 …을 가장 좋아해?

264 **Which do you like?**

어떤 걸 좋아해?

"어떤 걸 더 좋아해?"는 Which do you like better?

265 **Which do you prefer?**

어떤 걸 더 좋아해?

266 **Which do you recommend?**

어떤 걸 추천해?

recommend는 추천하다

267 **Which flight are you going to take?**

어떤 비행편을 탈거야?

268 **Which guy are you talking about?**

어떤 녀석을 말하는 거야?

269 **Which is better?**

어떤 게 더 나아?

270 **Which Mr. Kim do you want to talk to?**

어느 미스터 김과 통화하시겠어요?

271 **Which one is better for me?**

어느게 내게 좋을까?

Which one~ 앞에 언급된 명사를 재반복하지 않고 더 단순하게 말하는 방식으로 어떤 거?라는 의미

272 **Which one is your new boyfriend?**

누가 네 새로운 남친이야?

273 **Which one of you is getting married?**

너희들 중 누가 결혼해?

Which one of you~는 너희들 중 누가~

274 **Which one?**

어떤거?

275 **Which part?**

어떤 부분?

276 **Which train goes to New York?**

뉴욕으로 가는게 어느 열차죠?

277 **Which way is it?**

그건 어느 쪽에 있어?

"화장실이 어느 쪽에 있어?는 Which way is the bathroom?

278 **Which way is out?**

어느 쪽이 출구인가요?

279 **Which way is shorter?**

어느 길이 더 빨라?

280 **Which way**

어떤 길?, 어떤 방법?

281 **Who cares!**

알게 뭐람!, 무슨 상관야!, 누가 신경이나 쓴대!

= I don't care at all.

282 **Who did this to you?**

누가 너에게 이렇게 한거야?

Who가 주어로 쓰인 경우

283 **Who did you go out with last night?**

지난 밤에 누구랑 데이트했어?

go out with sb는 …와 데이트하다

284 **Who did you have lunch with?**

누구랑 점심했어?

have lunch with sb는 …와 함께 점심을 먹다

285 **Who do you hang out with?**

누구랑 어울려 놀아?

"그냥 나와 놀자"는 Just hang out with me.

286 **Who do you like?**

누굴 좋아해?

Who = Whom

287 **Who do you think is going to get married next?**

다음에 누가 결혼할 것 같아?

Who do you think+V~?, Who do you think S+V?는 누가 …할 거라고 생각해?

288 **Who do you think she's going to pick?**

걔가 누구를 고를 것 같아?

289 **Who do you think you are?**

(주로 싸울 때) 네가 도대체 뭐가 그리도 잘났는데?

= Why are you acting that way? "더 이상 내게 말도 안 하는데 네가 도대체 뭔데 그래?"는 You never talk to me anymore. Who do you think you are?

290 **Who do you think you're kidding?**

설마 나더러 그 말을 믿으라는 건 아니지

= You can't trick me

291 **Who do you think you're talking to?**

내가 그렇게 바보로 보여?

292 **Who do you want to hire?**

누구를 고용하고 싶어?

Who do you want to+V? 누구를 …하고 싶어?

293 **Who do you want to invite to the party?**

파티에 누굴 초대하고 싶어?

294 **Who do you want to speak to?**

누구랑 통화하시겠어요?

295 **Who do you work for?**

어디서 일해?

Who do you work for?에서는 Who가 동사구 work for의 목적어로 사용되었고, 의미는 누구을 위해 일하냐, 즉 어디서 일하냐라는 문장이다.

296 **Who is available now?**

누가 시간낼 수 있어?

297 **Who is it?**

(초인종이 울릴 때 혹은 전화왔다고 누가 말해줄 때) 누구세요?, 누군데?

"너 좋아하는 사람있지. 누군지 말해봐. 누구야?"는 You like someone. Tell me who it is. Who is it?

298 **Who is ready to go?**

갈 준비 된 사람?

299 **Who is this?**

(옆에 모르는 사람이 있을 때 혹은 전화에서) 이 사람 누구야? 누구시죠?

Who is this guy?는 이 친구 누구야?

300 **Who knows how to get there?**

누가 거기에 가는 방법을 알아?

Who knows how to+V?는 누가 …하는 방법을 알아?

301 **Who said I went there?**

내가 거기에 갔다고 누가 그래?

Who said S+V?는 누가 …라고 했어?

302 **Who said that I didn't like you?**

내가 널 좋아하지 않는다고 누가 그래?

303 **Who said that?**

누가 그래?

that 대신에 it을 써도 된다.

304 **Who told you?**

누가 그랬어?

Who told you that?이라고 해도 된다.

305 **Who took Wendy to the party?**

누가 웬디를 파티에 데려갔어?

take sb to the party는 …을 파티에 데려가다

306 **Who wants to go first?**

제일 먼저 가고 싶은 사람?

Who wants to+V?는 누가 …을 하고 싶어?

307 **Who wants to tell him the truth?**

걔에게 진실을 말해주고 사람?

tell sb the truth는 …에게 사실을 말하다

308 **Who was it?**

(상황종료 후 방문객이 누군인지 전화한 사람인 누군지 물어볼 때) 누군데? 누구였어?

"누구 만났구나! 누구였어?"는 You met someone! Who was it?

309 **Who went to the grocery?**

누가 식품점에 갔어?

Who went to+장소명사?는 누가 …에 갔어?

310 **Who's calling, please?**

(전화) 누구세요?

311 **Who's Dick?**

딕이 누구야?

312 **Who's going to go out tonight after work?**

오늘밤 퇴근 후에 회식자리에 누가 가?

Who's going to+V?는 누가 …할거야?

313 **Who's going to pay for this?**

누가 이거 낼거야?

pay for~는 …에 대한 값을 치루다

314 **Who's gonna give me a ride?**

누가 나 태워줄거야?

315 **Who's in charge?**

누가 책임자야

be in charge는 책임지다

316 **Who's next?**

다음은 누구야?

317 **Who's the guy next your mother?**

네 엄마 옆에 있는 사람 누구야?

318 **Why are you here?**

너 여기 왜 있는 거야?

319 **Why are you so angry?**

왜 그리 화났어?

"왜 그렇게 내게 화를 내는거야?는 Why are you so angry at me?

320 **Why did you do that?**

왜 그랬어?

= How could you do this[that]?

321 **Why did you hate me?**

왜 나를 싫어했어?

Why did you+V?는 왜 …했어?

322 **Why didn't I think of that?**

내가 왜 그걸 생각못했을까?

323 **Why didn't you call me last night?**

어젯밤에 왜 전화안했어?

Why didn't you+V?는 왜 …을 하지 않았어?

A-D E-H I-K L-P S-T U-W Y

324 **Why didn't you just tell her the truth?**

걔한테 진실을 왜 말하지 않았어?

325 **Why didn't you say anything?**

왜 아무 말도 하지 않았어?

326 **Why didn't you take the job?**

왜 그 일을 맡지 않았어?

take the job은 일자리를 맡기로 하다

327 **Why didn't you tell me?**

왜 내게 말하지 않았어?

328 **Why do I have to apologize?**

내가 왜 사과해야 돼?

Why do I have to+V?는 왜 내가 …해야 돼?

329 **Why do I have to tell her?**

내가 왜 걔에게 말해야 돼?

330 **Why do you care so much?**

왜 그렇게 신경 써?

331 **Why do you keep saying that?**

왜 계속 그렇게 말하는거야?

keep saying that은 계속 그렇게 말하다

332 **Why do you need it?**

왜 그게 필요한거야?

333 **Why do you say that?**

왜 그런 말을 해?, 어째서요?

Why would you say S+V?는 왜 …하다고 말하는거야?

334 **Why do you think I'm such a bad person?**

왜 내가 나쁜놈이라고 생각하는거야?

Why do you think S+V?는 왜 …라고 생각하는거야?

335 **Why do you think so?**

왜 그렇게 생각해?

A-D E-H I-K L-P S-T U-W Y

336 **Why do you think the economy is doing poorly?**

왜 경기가 나쁘다고 생각해?

337 **Why does everyone hate me so much?**

왜 다들 날 그렇게 싫어하는거야?

338 **Why don't I show you the baby's room?**

애기방 보여줄게

Why don't I~? = Let me~

339 **Why don't we invite her?**

걔를 초대하자

Whdy don't we~? = Let's~

340 **Why don't you come over here and talk to me for a second?**

이리와 나랑 잠시 얘기하자

Why don't you~ ?= I want you to+V

341 **Why don't you come with me?**

나랑 같이 가자

Why don't you+동사?는 무늬는 의문문이지만 실제로는 상대방에게 뭔가 제안을 하는 문장으로 이유와는 거리가 있다

342 **Why don't you get some rest?**

좀 쉬지 그래

get some rest는 좀 쉬다

343 **Why don't you give me all of the details?**

자세히 말 좀 해봐

give sb all of the details는 …에게 상세히 말하다

344 **Why don't you go find the mother and talk to her**

가서 엄마 찾아 얘기해

go find = go to[and] find

345 **Why don't you go see Frankie?**

가서 프랭키 만나보는 게 어때?

go see = go to[and] see

346 **Why don't you make up your mind?**

결정하지 그래

make up one's mind = decide

347 **Why don't you take a break?**

쉬지 그래

take a break은 잠시 쉬다

348 **Why don't you tell me what happened?**

무슨 일인지 내게 말해봐

349 **Why don't you try to relax, okay?**

좀 긴장을 풀어봐, 응?

350 **Why is he so unhappy?**

걘 왜 그렇게 기분이 안좋은거야?

상대방에게 이유를 물어보는 표현으로 Why is[are] you + 형용사[~ing/pp]~?의 형태로 쓰인다

351 **Why is it so hard to admit that?**

그걸 인정하는게 왜 그렇게 힘들어?

Why is it so+형용사+to+V?는 …하는게 왜 그렇게 힘들어?

352 **Why is it so important to you?**

그게 왜 네게 그렇게 중요해?

353 **Why is it that you're not coming?**

넌 왜 안오는거야?

Why is it that S+V?는 왜 …야?

354 **Why is that so hard to believe?**

그게 왜 그렇게 믿겨지지 않는거야?

355 **Why is this happening?**

왜 이런 일이 벌어지는 거야?

356 **Why not?**

그러지 뭐, 왜 안되는거야?

"왜 안돼? 좋은 기회인데"는 Why not? It's a good chance, "왜 걔는 안돼?"는 Why not her?

357 **Why should I protect her?**

내가 왜 걸 보호해야 돼?

Why should I+V?는 왜 내가 …해야 돼?

358 **Why the long face?**

왜 우울한 표정이야?

= Why do you seem so gloomy?

359 **Why was this door locked?**

이 문이 왜 잠겨져 있는거야?

A-D E-H I-K L-P S-T U-W Y

360 **Why would you say that?**

왜 그런 소리를 해?

= What made you talk that way?

361 **Will it be ready by one o'clock?**

한 시까지는 준비될까?

362 **Will that be all?**

더 필요한 건 없어요?

상점표현으로 다 고르셨나요? 더 필요한 건 없으시고요?라는 의미

363 **Will that be cash or charge?**

현금으로 내시겠어요, 아님 신용카드로 하시겠어요?

카드로 할게요는 Chage it, please, 현금으로 할게요는 Cash, please. 신용카드로 결제한다고 할 때는 I'd like to buy it on credit, 수표로 낼게요는 I'll pay by check

364 **Will that be everything?**

이게 전부입니까?

365 **Will you be able to attend?**

참석할 수 있어?

366 **Will you be here tomorrow afternoon?**

내일 오후에 여기 올거야?

367 **Will you calm down?**

좀 진정해라

calm down = relax = take it easy

368 **Will you come in here a moment?**

잠깐 좀 들어와봐

369 **Will you get me a ride home?**

집까지 태워다 줄래?

get sb a ride home는 집까지 차로 태워주다

370 **Will you have more coffee?**

커피 좀 더 들래요?

371 **Will you help me write a report?**

보고서 쓰는 거 좀 도와줄래?

write a report는 보고서를 쓰다

372 **Will you help me?**

나 도와줄래?

373 **Will you hold this for a sec?**

잠깐 이것 좀 들고 있어줘

for a sec = for a second = for a moment = for a minute

374 **Will you marry me?**

나하고 결혼해주겠니?

= Please spend your life with me. 청혼하다 = pop the question

375 **Won't you come in?**

들어오지 않을래?

376 **Would you all relax? It's not that big a deal**

모두 긴장 풀어라. 뭐 큰일 아니잖아.

377 **Would you come over here please?**

좀 이리로 와볼래요?

come over here는 이리로 오다

378 **Would you get that?**

문 좀 열어줄래, 전화 좀 받아줄래

= Can you open the door? or Can you pick up the phone?

379 **Would you go out with me?**

나랑 데이트할래요?

go out with = go on a date with

380 **Would you keep in touch with me?**

나하고 연락하고 지낼래요?

keep in touch with sb는 …와 연락하고 지내다

381 **Would you lend me some money?**

돈 좀 빌려줄래요?

lend sb some money는 …에게 돈을 좀 빌려주다

382 **Would you like an appetizer?**

애피타이저 드실래요?

Would you like +명사?의 경우는 I'd like+명사의 경우에서처럼 음식관련 상황에서 유용하게 쓰인다.

383 **Would you like me to do it?**

그게 내가 할까요?

Would you like me to+V?는 내가 …할까요?

384 **Would you like me to get out of here?**

여기서 나가줄까?

385 **Would you like me to go with you?**

너랑 같이 가자고?

386 **Would you like something to drink?**

마실 것 좀 줄까요?

387 **Would you like to come in?**

들어오실래요?

Would you like to+V?는 …할래?

388 **Would you like to go out to lunch with me?**

나랑 점심먹으러 갈래?

go out to lunch with sb는 나가서 …와 점심을 하다

389 **Would you like to go out with me sometime?**

언제 나하고 데이트할래?

390 **Would you like to go to a movie?**

영화 볼래?

391 **Would you like to have coffee?**

커피 드실래요?

392 **Would you like to try it on?**

한번 입어 보시겠어요?

try sth on은 입어보다, 신어보다

393 **Would you mind watching my bag for a moment?**

잠시 가방 좀 봐줄래요?

Would you mind ~ing?는 …해줄래요?

394 **Would you please be more specific?**

좀 더 정확하게 말해줄래요?

specific은 구체적인

395 **Would you please excuse me for a moment?**

잠시 실례해도 될까요?

396 **Would you recommend a good restaurant?**

좋은 식당 추천해줄래요?

397 **Would you speak a little louder?**

좀 크게 말해줄래요?

398 **Would you speak more slowly please?**

좀 천천히 말해 줄래요?

399 **Would you stop doing that?**

그만 좀 안 할래?

Will you ~?와 마찬가지로 Would you ~? 또한 억양을 바꾸면 명령에 가까운 요청의 문장이 된다.

400 **Would you turn the TV down?**

TV소리 좀 줄여줄래요?

turn down은 TV 등의 소리를 줄이다. 반대는 turn up.

CHECK IT OUT! 문장속에서 확인해보기!

A: That pizza was great.
B: Want some more?
A: I'd love another piece if there is any left.

A: 피자는 정말 맛있었어.
B: 좀 더 먹을래?
A: 남은 게 있으면 한 조각 더 먹었으면 좋겠는데.

★ I'd love~
I'd like sth과 같은 의미. 마찬가지로 I'd love to+V와 I'd like to+V는 같은 표현이다.

A: Guess what? I just got my test results back. I got the highest score in the class!
B: Way to go! I'm so proud of you.
A: Thanks. Me too!

A: 그거 알아? 지금 막 성적표를 받았는데. 내가 우리 반에서 제일 좋은 점수를 받았어!
B: 잘했구나! 네가 정말 자랑스러워.
A: 고마워. 나두 그래!

★ Guess what?
Guess what? 놀라운 사실을 언급하기 전에 「그거 알아?」라면서 운을 떼는 말.

A: What's eating you, Mom?
B: Oh, I'm just worried about your dad. He was supposed to be home a long time ago.
A: Maybe he's stuck in traffic.

A: 무슨 일이에요, 엄마?
B: 응, 아빠 걱정을 하고 있단다. 집에 벌써 왔어야 하는데.
A: 차가 막히는 모양이죠.

★ was supposed to
be supposed to+V는 실제 회화에서 무척 많이 쓰이는 표현으로 「…하기로 되어 있다」라는 의미이다.

A: Would you be interested in coming over for a barbecue tomorrow?
B: Tomorrow is not a good time. **Thanks anyway**, though.
A: Well, what about tonight? Are you busy?

A: 내일 바베큐 먹으러 올래요?
B: 내일은 좀 그런데요. 아무튼 고마워요.
A: 그럼 오늘 밤은요? 바쁜가요?

★what about
상대방의 의견을 묻거나 뭔가 제안하는 것으로 How about~으로 생각해도 된다.

A: Sorry, I couldn't understand what you just said.
B: **Would you like me to go over it again with you?**
A: Yes, if you don't mind.
B: No, I don't mind at all.

A: 미안해요. 방금 말한 걸 이해못했어요.
B: 다시 얘기해 드려요?
A: 네, 괜찮으시다면요.
B: 그럼요, 괜찮아요.

★if you don't mind
뭔가 제안하기에 앞서 하는 말로 「네가 괜찮다면」, 즉 I'd like you to~와 같은 의미이다.

A: Go to the store and get me something.
B: **Would you please be more specific?**
A: Sure, get me a can of Coke and some chocolate bars.

A: 가게에 가서 뭐 좀 사다 줘.
B: 좀더 구체적으로 얘기해줄래?
A: 그래, 콜라 하나랑 초콜릿 몇개 사다줘.

★get me
get sb sth은 「…에게 …을 가져다주다」, 혹은 「사주다」라는 의미이다.

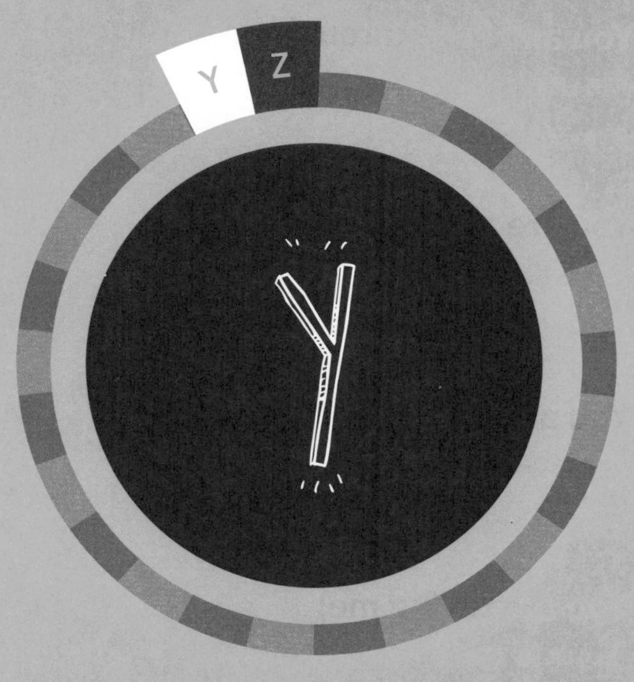
Y
Z
Y

Y

001 **You and I are through**

너와 난 끝났어

be through = be over

002 **You are always complaining**

넌 항상 불평이야

003 **You are always so generous**

넌 항상 관대해

generous는 관대한

004 **You are telling me!**

누가 아니래!, 나도 알아

= That is right or I know that. You're telling me (that) S +V는 …라고 말하는거야?

005 **You are the most beautiful woman in the room**

넌 이 방에서 제일 예뻐

006

You asked for it!

네가 자초한 일이잖아!

= Your actions caused this problem.

007

You can call me any time

언제라도 전화해

008

You can call me Chris

크리스라고 불러

call sb~는 …을 …라 부르다, call sb's name은 …의 이름을 부르다, call sb name은 …의 욕을 하다

009

You can count on me

내게 맡겨

"내가 옆에 있잖아. 항상 날 믿어"는 I'm here for you. You can always count on me.

010

You can do anything

너 뭐든 할 수 있어

011

You can feel free to use it

마음편히 그걸 사용해도 돼

feel free to+V는 맘편히 …하다

012 **You can go first**

네가 먼저 가

013 **You can go now**

이제 가도 돼

여기서 can은 허가

014 **You can have as many as you want**

네가 원하는 만큼 먹어

여기서 have는 먹다라는 동사

015 **You can say that again**

그렇고 말고, 정말 그래

= I agree with you

016 **You can trust me**

날 믿어봐

= I'm honest

017 **You can't be serious**

농담이겠지, 말도 안돼

= Are you kidding?

018 **You can't do anything yourself, can you?**

너 스스로 아무것도 못하지, 그지?

019 **You can't do that**

그러면 안돼

"아빠, 그러면 안돼요. 너무 불공평해요"는 Dad, you can't do that. This is so unfair.

020 **You can't do this to me**

내게 이러면 안되지, 이러지마

= I'm very unhappy about what you did.

021 **You can't help yourself**

너도 어쩔 수가 없잖아

022 **You can't miss it**

(길을) 쉽게 찾을 수 있을거예요

= It's easy to see.

023 **You can't trust people you meet on the Internet**

인터넷에서 만난 사람을 믿으면 안돼

024 **You can't believe how sorry I am**

뭐라 사과해야 할지 모르겠어

= I can't tell you how sorry I am

025 **You caught me**

들켰어

= You found I did a bad thing.

026 **You did a good job!**

아주 잘했어요!

= Your work was good.

027 **You did?**

그랬어?

= Really?

028 **You didn't answer my question**

내 질문에 답을 안했어

You didn't+V는 넌 …을 하지 않했어

029 **You didn't ask anything about him?**

걔에 대해 아무 것도 묻지 않았어?

030 **You didn't do anything, did you?**

너 아무 것도 안했지, 그지?

031 **You didn't even try!**

너 해보려고 하지도 않았잖아!

032 **You didn't say anything about that**

넌 그거에 관해 아무 말도 안했어

033 **You didn't seem so upset about it**

그 때문에 화나 보이지 않았어

seem upset about~는 ….에 화나다, 속상하다

034 **You didn't tell me your boyfriend smoked**

네 여자친구가 담배핀다는 얘기안했어

You didn't tell me S+V는 넌 내게 …을 말하지 않았어

035 **You don't care what I think, so I'm out of here!**

내 생각은 신경도 안 쓰잖아, 나 갈게!

You don't care what~ 은 넌 …을 신경쓰지 않다. "넌 걔가 뭘 필요로 하는지 상관없잖아"는 You don't care what she needs.

036

You don't have to be sorry

미안해 할 필요없어

You don't have to+V = You don't need to+V

037

You don't have to do that

그럴 필요 없어

038

You don't have to say you're sorry

미안하단 말은 할 필요없어

039

You don't have to walk me home

집까지 나하고 함께 걸어갈 필요없어

walk sb home은 …을 따라 집까지 걸어가다

040

You don't know how that happened?

그게 어떻게 그렇게 됐는지 모른단 말야?

041

You don't know me at all

넌 날 전혀 몰라

042 **You don't know what you're doing**

넌 네가 무얼 하는지도 몰라

You don't know what[how] S+V는 넌 …가 ~하는지 몰라

043 **You don't need to know**

알 필요없어

You don't need to+V = You don't have to+V

044 **You don't need to talk about it**

그거에 대해 말할 필요없어

045 **You don't need to worry about that**

그거 걱정할 필요없어

worry about~는 …을 걱정하다

046 **You don't say!**

설마!, 정말!

= Oh really?

047 **You don't seem okay**

안 좋아 보여

048 **You done?**

끝냈어?

= Have you finished? = Are you through?

049 **You don't even know her**

넌 걜 알지도 못하잖아

050 **You feel better now?**

좀 기분이 나아졌어?

051 **You go have fun.**

가서 재미있게 즐겨

052 **You got her to stop crying!**

걔가 우는 걸 그치도록 해!

get sb to+V는 …가 …하도록 하다

053 **You got it**

맞아. 알았어

You got it?은 알았어?, You got that?은 알아들었어?

054 **You got to get me some work**

일 좀 줘야죠

055 **You had it coming**

네가 자초한거야

= You asked for it = What happened was your fault.

056 **You have a good memory**

너 기억력 좋구나

You have+N은 넌 …하구나

057 **You have a nice home**

너 집이 좋구나

058 **You have a point**

네 말이 맞아

= You've got a point.

059 **You have a point there**

네 말이 맞아

= That idea is good.

060 **You have all my sympathy**

참 안되셨습니다

061 **You have gone too far**

네가 너무 했어

= Your behavior will get you in trouble this time. "내가 너무 했어"는 I have gone too far.

062 **You have my word**

내 약속할게

I give you my word S+V는 …을 약속할게

063 **You have no idea**

넌 몰라

064 **You have no idea how much I miss her**

내가 얼마나 걔를 그리워하는지 넌 모를거야

065 **You have no idea how much I need this**

이게 나한테 얼마나 필요한지 넌 몰라

You have no idea what[how]는 …을 넌 모를거야

066 **You have no idea what it's like to care for somebody**

다른 누군가를 좋아한다는게 뭔지 너는 몰라

You don't know[You have no idea] what it's like to~는 …하는 것이 어떤 건지 넌 몰라

067 **You have no idea what this means to me!**

이게 내게 얼마나 중요한 건지 넌 몰라!

068 **You have the wrong number**

전화 잘못거셨어요

= You made a mistake calling here = Sorry, wrong number.

069 **You have to be careful**

조심해야돼

070 **You have to get this done by Friday**

금요일까지 이거 끝내야 돼.

get sth done by+시간명사는 …때까지 …을 끝내다

071 **You have to get used to it**

적응해야지

get[be] used to+N은 …에 적응하다

072 **You have to go there right now**

지금 당장 거기에 가야 돼

You have to+V는 넌 …을 해야 돼

073 **You have to listen very carefully**

매우 신중히 이야기를 들어봐

074 **You have to look on the bright side**

긍정적으로 생각하라고

look on the bright side는 긍정적으로 보다

075 **You have to take care of yourself**

너 스스로를 돌봐야 돼

take care of oneself는 스스로를 돌보다

076 **You have to try harder**

더 열심히 해야 돼

try harder는 더 열심히 하다

077 **You have two new messages**

메시지가 두 개 와 있어요

078 **You haven't changed a bit**

넌 조금도 변하지 않았네

079 **You heard me**

내 말 명심해, 내가 말했지

= I meant it when I said~~

080 **You just wait and see**

두고 봐, 기다려 봐

"계속 무슨 일이 일어나는지 지켜볼거야"는 We are going to just continue to wait and see what happens.

081 **You keep looking at me. Do you have a problem with me?**

날 계속 쳐다보는데 뭐 불만있어?

082 **You know what I like most about him, though?**

그래도 걔한테서 가장 좋아하는 게 뭔지 알아?

083 **You know what I mean?**

내 말 무슨 말인지 알지?

= Do you understand my idea?

084 **You know what I'm saying?**

내 말이 무슨 말인지 알겠어?

085 **You know what makes me mad?**

뭐가 날 열받게 하는지 알아?

You know what makes sb~? …가 뭣 때문에 …는지 알아?

086 **You let me know if you can**

가능한 지 알려줘

087 **You like baseball?**

야구 좋아해?

088 **You like comic books, right?**

만화책 좋아하지, 맞지?

089 **You like to play games, John?**

존, 너 게임하는거 좋아하지?

You like to+V?는 넌 …하기를 좋아하지?

090 **You look great**

너 멋져 보인다

"너 행복해 보여"는 You look happy, "너 창백해 보여"는 You look pale.

091 **You look so depressed**

너 우울해보여

depressed = 우울한 = gloomy

092 **You look stressed out**

스트레스에 지쳐보여

be stressed out = be worn out = be tired out = be washed out

093 **You look tired**

너 피곤해보여

094 **You look young for your age**

네 나이에 비해 어려 보여

095 **You love this, don't you?**

너 이거 좋아하지, 그렇지 않아?

096 **You made her cry!**

네가 걔를 울렸어!

097 **You made it**

너 해냈구나.

I made it은 쉽지 않은 일을 해내다

098 **You made me feel like an idiot**

너 때문에 바보가 된 기분이야

"너 나를 바보로 만드는구나"는 You make me feel like a loser.

099 **You make me feel much better**

네 덕분에 기분이 한결 낫구나

make somebody feel like~는 …을 …처럼 느끼게 하다

100 **You make me happy**

네가 있어 행복해

"너 때문에 짜증난다"는 You make me sick.

101 **You may go now**

가도 돼

허락의 may

102 **You may have a cancer**

암일지도 모릅니다

추측의 may

103 **You may have heard of it**

아마 들어본 적이 있을 거야

may have+pp는 과거에 …을 했을지도 모른다

104 **You mean it?**

정말야?,

mean it은 진심이다, 정말이다

105 **You mean she hasn't called you and told you yet?**

걔가 아직 전화해서 말하지 않았단 말야?

You mean~하게 되면 내가 상대방의 말을 이해못했거나 헷갈릴 경우 상대방이 한 말을 확인하고자 할 때 쓰는 표현

106 **You mean you're not going to come over?**

못 온다는 말이지?

107 **You mean, when you were a baby**

네 말은 네가 애기였을 때 말이지

108 **You mean, you and me?**

네 말은 너와 나랑 말야?

109 **You might be true**

네 말이 맞을지도 몰라

might be~는 추측

110 **You must be new here**

여긴 잘 모르시겠네요

You must be~는 추측으로 …임에 틀림없다. "오웬이시죠"는 You must be Owen.

111 **You must be tired**

너 피곤하겠구나

"맘 상했겠구나"는 You must be upset.

112 **You must be very proud**

무척 자랑스러우시겠어요

113 **You must go there**

넌 거기에 가야 돼

must는 have to와 더불어 강한 추측의 조동사

114 **You must have been hungry**

배고팠겠구만

must have+pp는 …했겠구나

115 **You must not go in there**

거기 들어가면 안돼

You must not+V는 넌 …해서는 안돼

116 **You must not make a noise**

시끄럽게 해서는 안돼

make a noise는 시끄럽게 하다

117 **You must work hard**

열심히 일해야 한다

work hard 열심히 일하다

118 **You mustn't think like that**

그렇게 생각하면 안돼

119 **You name it**

말만해

= Whatever you want will be done.

120 **You need to keep practicing**

계속 연습을 해야 한다

You need to+V는 넌 …해야 해

121 **You never talk about your wife. What's she like?**

네 아내 얘기 한 적이 없어. 어떤 사람야?

You never talk about~은 넌 …대해 말한 적이 없어

122 **You probably feel like you don't have a chance**

아마 기회가 없다고 느낄지도 몰라

123 **You really can't stand to lose, can you?**

넌 지는 걸 못참지, 그지?

can't stand to~는 …을 참지 못하다

124 **You really take after your mother**

넌 정말 네 엄마를 닮았어

take after = resemble

125 **You remember him, don't you?**

넌 걔 기억하지, 그렇지 않아?

126 **You said it was going to be fun**

재미있을 거라고 했잖아

You said S+V는 앞에 있는 사람보고 …라고 말하지 않았냐? …라고 했잖아라는 말로 상대방이 한 말을 재확인하거나 상황에 따라 따지는 문장

127 **You said it was okay**

괜찮다고 했잖아

128 **You said that**

네가 그랬잖아

129 **You said you wanted to talk about it**

넌 그거에 대해 얘기하고 싶다고 했잖아

130 **You said you were sick of this**

이건 지겹다고 했잖아

be sick of = be tired of

131 **You see that?**

내 말이 맞지?, 내 그럴 줄 알았어

= Look, I knew that would happen.

132 **You seem a little down**

좀 우울해 보여

be a little down는 좀 쳐저 보인다

133 **You seem a little nervous**

너 좀 초조해보여

134 **You should do it at once**

곧 그것을 해야지

at once는 곧

135 **You should do that**

그렇게 하도록 해

should는 약한 의무 = ought to

136 **You should speak to your teacher**

선생님에게 말해라

137 **You should take a rest**

너 좀 쉬는 게 좋아 보여

take a rest는 쉬다

138 **You should take a subway**

전철을 타

take a subway는 전철을 타다

139 **You shouldn't be here**

넌 여기 오면 안돼

You shouldn't+V ~하게 되면 상대방에게 충고나 금지할 때 쓰는 표현으로 하지 마라, …하지 않는 게 좋겠어라는 뜻

140 **You shouldn't blame yourself for this**

이걸로 널 자책하지마

blame oneself for~는 …로 자책하다

141 **You shouldn't go there**

거기 가지 마라

142 **You shouldn't have come here**

넌 여기에 오지 말았어야 하는데

shouldn't have+pp은 …을 하지 말았어야 했는데 과거에 그렇게 했다

143 **You shouldn't have done this**

이럴 필요까지는 없는데(특히 선물을 받을 때)

You shouldn't have라고 해도 된다. 의미는 그럴 필요 없는데, (선물 받으면서) 이러지 않아도 되는데.

144

You shouldn't lie on your resume

이력서에 거짓말을 해서는 안돼

lie on one's resume는 이력서에 허위사실을 기재하다

145

You shouldn't talk to your mother like that

어머니한테 그렇게 말하면 안돼

talk to sb like that은 그런 식으로 …에게 얘기하다

146

You shouldn't treat me like this way

날 이런 식으로 대하면 안돼

treat sb like this way는 …을 이런 식으로 대하다

147

You shouldn't be starting rumors

넌 소문을 퍼뜨리면 안돼

start rumors는 소문을 퍼뜨리다

148

You sound strange

네 목소리가 이상하게 들려

149

You take her to lunch and have her get dessert

걔한테 점심하고 디저트를 사줘

have sb+V는 …가 …하도록 하다

150 **You told me Jane was pregnant**

네가 제인이 임신했다고 했잖아

You told me (that) S+V 혹은 You told me to~는 네가 …라고 했잖아라는 의미로 상대방이 예전에 한 말을 다시 되새김할 때

151 **You told me you liked it**

네가 좋다고 했잖아

152 **You told me you were going to take me for lunch**

나 점심 사준다고 했잖아

153 **You turn me on**

널 보면 흥분돼

turn sb on은 …을 흥분시키다

154 **You two need to be nice to each other**

사이 좋게 지내야 돼

155 **You were a great help**

정말 많은 도움이 되었어요

A-D E-H I-K L-P S-T U-W Y

156 **You were both aware of the situation**

너희 둘 모두 상황을 알고 있었잖아

be aware of~는 …을 알고 있다

157 **You will be in trouble**

넌 난처하게 될거야

"그렇게 하면 곤란해질거야"는 You will get in trouble if you do that.

158 **You will get to know that**

그걸 알게 될거야

get to+V는 …하게 되다

159 **You will never see me again**

날 다시는 못보게 될거야

You will never+V는 넌 절대로 …하지 못할거야

160 **You won't regret this**

넌 이걸 후회하지 않을거야

161 **You won't believe this**

이거 믿지 못할 걸

= This is very surprising = You're not gonna believe this.

162 **You'd better be careful**

조심해라

You have better+V = You'd better+V = You better+V = Better+V

163 **You'd better be on time tomorrow**

내일 늦지 않도록 해라

be on time은 제시간에 오다

164 **You'd better do it now**

그거 당장 하는 게 좋을 걸

"지금 바로 이거 해"는 You'd better do it right now.

165 **You'd better get used to it**

적응하도록 해라

You'd better+동사는 보통 친구나 아랫사람에게 하는 말로 …해라, …하는 게 좋을 것이라는 뜻으로 충고내지는 문맥에 따라서는 경고로도 쓰인다.

166 **You'd better hurry**

서둘러라

167 **You'd better not use my hair dryer**

내 헤어드라이어기 쓰지 마라

You'd better not+V는 …하지 마라

168 **You'd better run it by me first**

나하고 상의해라

run A by B는 B에게 A에 대한 상의를 하다, A를 허락받기 위해 B에게 설명하다. "다시 한번 말(설명)해달라"는 Run it[that] by me again.

169 **You'll be sorry if you're late again**

또 늦으면 후회하게 될거야

상대방에게 경고나 주의를 줄 때 사용하는 표현. You'll be sorry about~ 혹은 You'll be sorry if S+V의 형태로 쓰이며 about이나 if 이하에 하면 안 되는 행동을 말하면 된다.

170 **You'll be sorry later**

나중에 후회할거야

171 **You'll get a better job**

좋은 직업을 갖게 될거야

172 **You'll get a discount if you pay in cash**

현찰로 지불하시면 할인받습니다

get a discount는 할인을 받다, pay in cach는 현찰로 지불하다

173 **You'll have to excuse me**

정말 죄송한데요

174 **You'll make a lot of money**

돈을 많이 벌 거야

make a lot fo money는 돈을 많이 벌다

175 **You're a really nice guy**

넌 정말 좋은 친구야

176 **You're almost there**

거의 끝났어!

= It's nearly over. be almost there는 목표지점에 거의 다다르다, 일을 거의 다 끝마치다

177 **You're dead wrong**

넌 완전히 틀렸어

"내가 말한 거 미안해. 내가 완전히 틀렸어"는 I'm so sorry about what I said. I was dead wrong.

178 **You're doing great**

잘하고 있어

"아주 잘하고 있어. 계속 해"는 You're doing great. Keep going.

179 **You're driving me crazy**

너 때문에 미치겠어

drive sb crazy는 …을 돌게 하다, 미치게 하다

180 **You're excited about going shopping**

넌 쇼핑가는 거에 들떠 있어

You're excited about~ing는 넌 …하는거에 신나있어

181 **You're fired**

넌 해고야

be fired = get fired

182 **You're here to see Susan?**

수잔보러 왔어?

183 **You're invited to Bob's bachelor party**

밥의 총각파티에 초대받았어

be invited to~는 …에 초대받다

184 **You're just saying that**

괜한 소리지

= I don't believe you.

185 **You're kidding me**

농담마

= That sounds like a joke.

186 **You're lucky**

너 운 좋다

187 **You're lying to me**

너 내게 거짓말하고 있지

lie to sb는 …에게 거짓말하다

188 **You're making a mistake**

너 실수하고 있는 거야

make a mistake는 실수하다

189 **You're making fun of me?**

날 놀리는거야?

make fun of sb는 …을 놀리다

190 **You're my best friend**

넌 나의 가장 친한 친구야

191 **You're not allowed to smoke here**

여기서 담배피면 안돼

You're not allowed to+V는 넌 …해서는 안돼

192
You're not listening

너 내 말 안듣고 있지

"내 말 안 듣는 것 같으네"는 You don't seem to be listening.

193
You're right about that

당신 말이 맞아요

be right about~는 …에 대해 맞다

194
You're scaring me

너 때문에 놀랐잖아

scare는 타동사로 …을 놀라게 하다

195
You're such a kind person

당신은 정말 친절하시군요

"넌 정말 요리를 잘해"는 You're such a good cook.

196
You're talking too much

넌 말이 너무 많아

197
You're ten times prettier than she is

네가 걔보다 10배나 예뻐

"넌 정말 멋진 여자야"는 You're the most wonderful girl.

198 **You're the best**

네가 최고야

199 **You're the one who ended it, remember?**

그걸 끝낸 건 너야, 기억해?

You're the one who~는 …한 것은 바로 너야

200 **You're welcome**

천만에, 무슨 말씀을

강조하려면 You're very welcome.

201 **You're welcome to come back any time**

언제라도 오면 환영야

You're welcome to+V는 편히 …해라

202 **You've been in love before?**

전에 사랑해본 적 있어?

203 **You've got a meeting at three**

3시에 회의 있어요.

You've got~ = You have

204

You've got nothing to lose

밑져야 본전이야

= You risk nothing

205

You've got to be kidding!

농담말아, 웃기지마

= That seems crazy

206

You've never been to New York?

뉴욕에 가본 적이 없지?

207

You're excused

그러세요, 괜찮아요, 그만가봐

Can you excuse us?라는 물음에 대한 답

208

You're not yourself

너 좀 이상해

= You see odd today.

209

You've got it all wrong

네가 잘못 알고 있는거야

= Your ideas are not right.

CHECK IT OUT! 문장속에서 확인해보기!

A: Thanks for the lovely dinner party.
B: **You're very welcome.** How about some dessert?
A: Well, I think I'd better be going now.

A: 아주 멋진 저녁 파티였어요.
B: 별 말씀을요. 디저트 좀 드실래요?
A: 저, 그만 가봐야 될 것 같아요.

★ I think I'd better be going
어서 일어나 자리를 떠나야겠다는 뉘앙스의 표현.

A: What are you doing for the next twenty minutes?
B: Actually, I must go now.
A: Oh, that's right… **you've got a meeting at three.**

A: 앞으로 20분 동안 뭐 할 겁니까?
B: 실은 그만 가야 돼요.
A: 어, 그래요. 3시에 회의가 있죠.

★ Actually
상대방의 예상과 어긋하는 말을 할 때 사용하는 것으로 「실은」, 「사실은」이라고 생각하면 된다.

A: **You look stressed out.** What's wrong?
B: I've got so much to do and I have to go now.
A: Let me help you.

A: 스트레스에 지쳐 빠진 것 같으네. 무슨 일이야?
B: 해야 할 일이 너무 많아서 지금 가야돼.
A: 내가 도와줄게.

★ I've got
I have = I have got이 성립하는 경우는 have의 의미가 「…을 갖고 있다」라는 의미일 경우에만 가능하다. 다시 말해서 have lunch= have got lunch는 성립되지 않는다는 말이다.

A: Kevin, what are you doing on Saturday night?
B: I'm not sure, why?
A: **You're invited to** Bob's bachelor party. We hope you'll be able to join us.

A: 케빈, 토요일 밤에 뭐해?
B: 잘 모르겠는데, 왜?
A: 밥의 총각파티에 참석했으면 해서. 올 수 있으면 좋겠는데.

★be able to~
can의 미래는 be able to~를 대신해서 표현한다.

A: Please accept my sincere apologies.
B: **Your apology is accepted.**
A: By the way, what are you doing tonight?

A: 제발 내 진심어린 사과를 받아줘요.
B: 다 용서했어요.
A: 근데, 오늘 밤에 뭐하실 거예요?

★By the way
화제를 바꿀 때 쓰는 표현으로 「근데 말야」라는 의미

A: **You don't have to say you're sorry.**
B: Sure I do. It was all my fault.
A: That's true, but it was an accident, wasn't it?

A: 미안하단 말은 할 필요 없어요.
B: 어떻게 그래요. 이게 다 제 잘못인데.
A: 그렇긴 해도 그건 우연한 사고였잖아요.

★Sure I do
여기서 do는 have to say I'm sorry라는 뜻이다.